TRIBAL IDENTITY AND MINORITY STATUS

About the Authors

Rudolf C. Heredia completed his Doctorate in sociology from the University Chicago in 1979. From 1980 he has been Director at the Social Science Centre at St. Xavier's College, Bombay, except for a brief spell in the Research Department of the Indian Social Institute, New Delhi, in 1992-94. His publications include:

Structure and Performance of College Education: An Organizational Analysis of Arts and Sciences in Bombay (Somaiya Bombay, 1981); "Religious and Social Change: Behavioral Responses in Bombay University" (Indian Social Institute, 1984); *Voluntary Action and Development: Toward a Praxis for Non-government Agencies* (Concept, 1988); *Urban Housing and Voluntary Agencies: Case Studies in Bombay* (Institute of Social Science, New Delhi 1989): *Tribal Education for Community Development: A Study of Schooling in the Talasair Mission Area* (Concept, 1992).

Rahul Srivastava graduated from St. Xavier's. College, Bombay University in Sociology in 1989. He completed his M.A. at Jawaharlal Nehru University, New Delhi, in 1991. After a year of teaching at St. Xavier College, he joined Social Science Centre to work on his research project. He is now an Inlaks scholar completing his M.Phil in social anthropology at Cambridge, England.

TRIBAL IDENTITY AND MINORITY STATUS

The Kathkari Nomads in Transition

RUDOLF C. HEREDIA
RAHUL SRIVASTAVA

CONCEPT PUBLISHING COMPANY PVT. LTD.
NEW DELHI-110059

ISBN: 978-81-7022-550-8

Edition 2025

Published and Printed by

Concept Since 1974

Concept Publishing Company Pvt. Ltd.
A/15-16, Commercial Block, Mohan Garden,
New Delhi-110059 (India)
T: 91-11-41101460
E: publishing@conceptpub.com, *W*: www.conceptpub.com

PREFACE

This study was undertaken as a collaborative venture between the Social Science Centre of St. Xavier's College and Janahit Vikas Trust (JVT), a church related NGO working since 1989 in Raigad (sometimes spelt Raigarh) district Maharashtra. By 1992, the year this study was begun, it had established a presence in the district through a variety of works. The purpose of this collaboration was to facilitate the reflection dimension of these works, to evolve an action-reflection process in an on-going praxis.

Since much of the work of the Janahit Vikas was with the Kathkaris of the area, a study of these tribals was undertaken. It was felt that any positive intervention on behalf of these marginalised and impoverished people must begin with a deep and empathetic understanding of their situation. However, precious little has been written on this small tribe and their dramatically changing circumstances today. Yet their situation is painfully familiar with many vulnerable people who are being swept away by an inequitous and alien development. Studying one such case in some depth will hopefully make for a more enlightened and effective response to other such groups trapped in a seemingly hopeless downward spiral.

Our gratitude is due to all our collaborators in the field and our supporters nearer home, but most especially to Frederick Sopena, the executive director of the JVT, on whose enthusiasm and optimism this study has 'limped' its way through to an enriching, enlightening and an ennobling experience.

Social Science Centre
St.Xavier's College
Bombay, June 1993

RUDOLF C. HEREDIA
RAHUL SRIVASTAVA.

CONTENTS

Map. Maharashtra District Raigarh
Source : Govt. of Maharashtra Publications

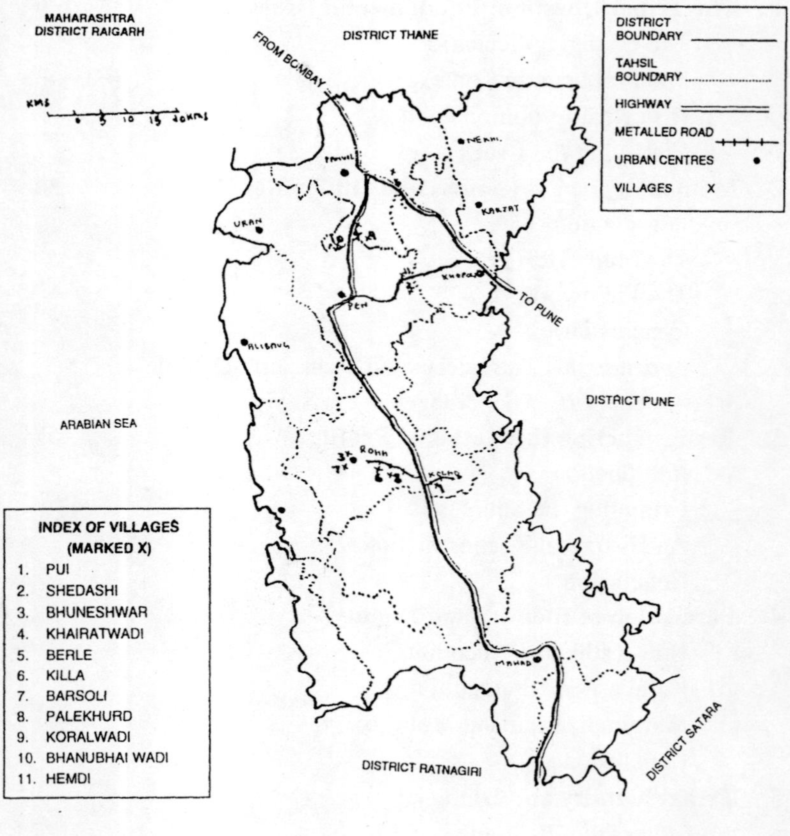

1

THE TRIBAL QUESTION: FUNDAMENTAL ISSUES

THE CHANGING SCENARIO

In a changing society, collective identities needs must change, and the deeper the change in one, the correspondingly deeper the change in the other will be. However, not all groups are equally or similarly affected by the change. Dominant groups more in control of their circumstances, would tend to come off more positively, just as subordinate groups more affected by than effecting their situation tend to come out negatively. In fact, the progress or development of some groups seems to correspond to the regress or 'the development of underdevelopment' in others, to use Andre Gunder Frank's phrase.[1] This happens not only in the world system or inter-nationally, but also within a particular national system or intra-nationally. For, whenever there are unequal relations of exchange between two groups, dominance-dependence relationships are inevitable.

Processes

In the rapid and radical changes that are sweeping through India, the tribals, variously called *adivasis, adimjatis, vanyajatis, vanvasis, grijans, pahadias,* etc., are clearly a very vulnerable group. Their identity as a tribal people is in effect negated, and their dignity as human persons all too often violated. Obviously, there is a connection between these two aspects of tribal life today: their marginalization from the benefits of development and their relegation to the bottom of the social hierarchy. For it is the same process of change that first isolates tribals, negating their identity and denigrating their dignity, and then integrates and assimilates them in a "forced division of labour", to use this phrase in the Durkheimian sense, into the lowest social strata, as alienated, anomic, violated persons, without rights or dignity in our society. Efforts to reverse this process have often been ineffective or even counter-productive.

Responses

A relevant response to the tribal situation in our changing world must begin with more than just benign goodwill and paternalistic benevolence. As people, they must be studied in their historical context, and perceived in relation to their environment. Once the 'tribal question' itself is thus clarified and contextualized, only then can the responses to it be usefully described and critiqued.

It is a truism to say that a solution to a problem depends very much on how the problem itself is defined. Here too, the perception of tribal identity has varied from romantic eulogizing to ethnocentric denigration. The responses, likewise, have covered the spectrum from romanticizing the primitivism of the 'noble savage' to assimilation into the mainstream, or even outright annihilation. What seems to be given less attention than it really deserves, is their human dignity and rights as tribals, or for that matter, as a vulnerable and disadvantaged group being overtaken by the maelstrom of social change. It would seem to us that this approach would make for a more critical perspective and a more human response.

Focusing

This study focuses on the Kathkaris, a small group of tribals in Raigad district, Maharashtra, near New Bombay. They are officially classified at different times as 'primitive' and 'economically backward'.[2] The floodtide of change just a small step away from their settlements represents for them a giant leap into an unfamiliar and unaccommodating world that threatens not just their Kathkari identity, but even their survival as a social group. Indeed, the tide of change will not leave them behind, it will sink them if they do not swim with it.

It is precisely because these Kathkari tribals are so vulnerable and so much at risk that a study of their changing situation in its historical context can provide a pertinent perspective from the 'underside', on these very changes. This, of course, would need to be complemented with views from other sides as well, to give a more complete picture of the various processes involved. However, in focusing on the Kathkaris, this study sets for itself a more modest agenda.

In this chapter we will begin descriptively with a sketch of the historical evolution of tribes in India. This will provide the context in which to review responses and initiatives that the various agencies, and the tribals themselves have made to their evolving situation. We can then proceed towards clarifying the more pertinent issues to be taken up in our study of the Kathkaris.

THE PROBLEMATIC CONTEXT

When the conceptual terms to be used in a study are defined at the outset, they implicitly set up a frame of reference within which the data is sought, and into which the conclusions must fit. If this framework is too narrow, it may exclude much that is pertinent, if it is too broad it may include much that is irrelevant. Yet any meaningful discussion must take place within a frame of reference, that is accessible to the discussant and relevant to the subject. This becomes specially pertinent when the subject is complex and the approaches to it are diverse. Even when it is limited to the Indian context, the anomalies associated with the term 'tribe', make it somewhat problematic. These cannot be ignored, but we can try to sort them out.

Towards a Definition

The etymological origin of the word tribe goes back to the Latin 'tribus', which referred to the three original divisions of the early Romans, and which has then been extended to any similar division whether of natural or political origin. Today the ordinary meaning of the word in the Oxford Dictionary is a "group of people in a primitive or barbarous stage of development acknowledging the authority of a chief and usually regarding themselves as having a common ancestor."[3] More recently the *International Encyclopaedia of the Social Sciences* suggests that "the unnecessary moralistic overtones that this usage implies can be minimized by the use of the expression 'tribal society'".[4] The word tribe still denotes "a teritorially defined political unit"[5] and has been defined more neutrally, but rather restrictively, as "a social group, usually with a defined area, dialect, cultural homogeneity, and unifying social organization."[6]

However, in ancient Indian literature there is really no equivalent word. The early Sanskrit references are to 'janas' or 'people'. "Prior to the British annexation, most of the presently called tribes were either unconscious of their ethnic identity or called themselves as 'people', *vis-a-vis* outsiders, in their own distinctive speech."[7] It was the British who designated these people as tribes, to distinguish them from Hindus and Muslims, since they were considered to be 'animists'. The other indigenous terms in use today are all of Sanskritic origin and coined rather recently by outsiders who worked with the tribals.[8]

The veteran anthropologist Stephen Fuchs categorically affirms, that "in fact, there exists no satisfactory definition of the term 'tribe' anywhere".[9] Since there is no common agreement on a substantive definition of the term anthropologists and others have fallen back on listing group characteristics to identify a people as 'tribals'. But more often than not these lists themselves serve better to illustrate the prejudices and presumptions of the compilers, than to make any, but a very tenuous, and sometimes even arbitrary, delineation between tribals and non-tribals in this country.

Thus the Report of the Commissioner for Scheduled Castes and Scheduled Tribes in 1952 listed eight characteristic tribal features: isolation in forests and hills; Negrito, Austroloid, or Mongoloid, racial stock; tribal dialect; animism; primitive occupations; carnivorous diet; naked or semi-naked attire, "nomadic habits" and "love of drink and dance".[10] T. B. Naik proposed seven characteristics to recognize a tribe: "functional interdependence", "economically backward", "geographically isolated", "common dialect", "common tribal authority", "averse to change", "its own traditional laws".[11] According to Piarey Lal Metha, "most popular definitions of the term tend to see in the tribes some, if not all the following characteristics: "original" or "at least some of the oldest inhabitants of the land", "relative isolation of the hills and forests", "shallow" sense of history; "low level of techno-economic development", distinctive "cultural ethics, language, institutions, belief and customs", "egalitarian" or "at least non-hierarchical and undifferentiated"[12].

An Ethnic Category

These lists can be multiplied, but already from the ones presented it is evident how they only compound rather than clarify the controversy. For the tribes in this country are in transition; they are at various stages of development and at different velocities of change. In such a situation any list of common features are bound to be ambiguous. Many of the scheduled tribes would not meet all the criteria and others not in the list would meet many of them.[13] Moreover, tribes can no longer be defined without reference to other groups in our society, especially scheduled castes and other subaltern groups. What we are left with then is a description of an ethnic category which we must distinguish from other ethnic groups by demarcating a community boundary, natural or constructed, that however permeable and tenuous, will still help towards a meaningful identification of such groups.[14]

But then urgent administrative requirements do not wait on the leisurely resolution of scholarly controversies. Already the Indian Legislative Council in 1916 decided that criminal and wandering tribes, aboriginal tribes, and untouchables be included in the term "Depressed

Classes". The 1931 Census separated out the tribals under the category of "Primitive Tribes" instead of "Forest Tribes" as in the 1891 Census or "Hill Tribes" in subsequent ones. In 1941 the Census used just "tribes", and today the Constitution of India refers to them as "Scheduled Tribes". The list notified in 1950 was revised in 1956 by the Backward Classes Commission following the reorganization of the states.

The Constitution nowhere attempts a substantive definition of the term 'tribe'. But it did try to set down a method and a machinery for designating tribals[15]. However, what the Commissioner for Scheduled Castes and Scheduled Tribes underlined in 1952 still remains true:

> No such uniform test has however, been evolved for classifying Scheduled Tribes with the result that in view of the divergent opinions held by Census authorities and public men from time to time, difficulties have been experienced in determining as to which tribe can rightly be included or excluded from the Scheduled Tribes. I consider that some definite criteria for this purpose must also be devised so that full justice is done at the time of respecification of the 'Scheduled Tribes'.[16]

Yet no such 'just criterion' has been devised and it is political pressures rather than social justice that has been at work in the revisions of this schedule. Thus in 1950 there were 212 Scheduled Tribes, by the 1981 Census, after two revisions of the list in 1956 and 1976, there were 427, comprising 7.76 per cent of the population, or 51.6 million people. As yet "however, ethonographic data on a number of tribal communities are lacking".[17]

An Ideological Concept

In other words, "tribe has clearly become an ideological concept, a concept which fails to recognize the reality it expresses."[18] As such, it could be expected that like 'race', as a concept, "the tribe would become redundant in academic discourse," except where it has remained politically "useful to the powers that be to manipulate divisions and rule over their subjects."[19]

Today "for almost all Indian researchers a tribe is a tribe which is included in the list of Scheduled Tribes".[20] But such a reduction of the term to a political administrative category, leaves out the socio-cultural dimensions, not to mention the economic one as well. This amounts to a fatal truncation for any relevant perspective on the tribals. Obviously another approach is called for. We believe the historical evolutionary one to be more promising.

HISTORICAL EVOLUTION

A Dynamic Perspective

The importance of an historical perspective in tribal studies has not always been conceded. Too easily this has been dismissed because "the documented referent was missing".[21] Due to their isolation the limited world view of the tribals was said to be characterized by lack of historical depth, where history merged into mythology.[22] Unfortunately, little effort has been made to use oral history, mostly because of the "ignorance on the part of the historian-ethnographer to interpret folklore metaphors and symbols for tracing the past of the people".[23]

This has lead to a static view of tribal society, and it gets increasingly out of sync as the pace of change among these people quickens. For "tribal society like any other society is not static. It has its own dynamism, it has its own history."[24] More recently, however, "the treatment of tribes as changing aggregates is an important departure from the orthodox beliefs in tribal research",[25] and a much overdue one too. In fact, in the rapid transition that all tribes are undergoing, each has its own history and stage of evolution, from food-gatherers and hunters, to shifting and settled cultivators, from pastoral nomads to urban-industrial workers. Any study of the tribals, then, must situate the group within the context of its evolutionary history.

The Pre-British Era

However, there are very limited sources on the tribals from the pre-British era, and these are from the dominant non-tribals, whose negative perception of these people and their habitat becomes quite evident. A century ago, J. Forsyth wrote how all the accounts from earlier times of these hill and forest dwellers—

> were filtered through Hindu and Mohmedan subordinates, whose horror of a jungle, and its unknown terrors, of bad air and general discomfort is such as to ensure their painting the country and its people in the blackest of colours.[26]

Hence these sources must be balanced against what we know or can conjecture from elsewhere.

The Sanskrit word 'jana' referred to non-monarchical societies outside the jati system. However, Ghurye insists that these tribes are not autochthonous societies but "in reality Backward Hindus", not quite properly integrated into Hindu society as yet.[27] Interestingly he thinks that "the Kathkaris of Maharashtra may be taken as the best representative of the smaller tribes getting assimilated without engendering violent conflicts."[28] Ghurye's perception seems to emphasize the tribes' assimilation into the jati system, unless one can think of the Hinduism as we know it, without caste.

It is this process of economic assimilation that N. K. Bose, called "the Hindu mode of absorption".[29] D.D. Kosambi suggests a brahminical model for this, especially through plough agriculture that replaced food-gathering and shifting cultivation and turned the nomadic tribe into a peasant caste.[30]

But there are severe limitations to this model. For other castes too were involved in this technological diffusion, especially artisan and peasant communities. Moreover, the 'sanskritization' process, first explained in cultural terms by Suniti Kumar Chatterji,[31] and later in a structural sense by M. N. Srinivas,[32] would have absorbed tribal and other subaltern communities into "a far more homogeneous pattern of culture through thousands of years of intergroup interaction",[33] than what actually has happened.

Yet some would insist that even if the brahmanic model is an inadequate explanation, still "the direction of tribal change is clear and predictable....towards jati characteristics".[34] Indeed, during this period some janas could well have been completely absorbed into the jati system. For as A. R. Desai writes: "A study of the history of the Indian civilization reveals how the growth and expansion of the Hindu society was a prolonged and complex process of assimilation, both forcible and peaceful, of the tribal people into it.... In fact, as history discloses various methods of tribal assimilation or absorption have been adopted in different societies in different epochs."[35]

Surely, tribes have been transformed into castes in many varied situations. For "the entire course of Indian history shows tribal elements being fused into a general society".[36] But then these people cease being tribal. Yet at the end of this period the British still find communities outside the caste system, though mostly isolated ones in more remote areas, whom they called tribes. For the janas that retained their culture, and consequently their tribal identity, could not be absorbed into the rigid jati hierarchy. Probably their geographic isolation did help as well.

In fact, all through the pre-British period "the forest dwelling people served as bridge or buffer communities between kingdoms".[37] It was this buffer role that made possible the autonomy needed for "the persistence of tribal communities as distinct entities, without forming themselves into organised states".[38] In this, tribal communities were essentially different from caste entities. For as long as the contact kingdoms needed a buffer "state intervention in the socio-cultural processes of the tribes"[39] would have been self-defeating. It was not in their interests to penetrate into tribal territory or assimilate tribal society. But with the coming of the British all this changed.

The Colonial Period

However exaggerated it might be to speak of 'frictionless coexistence' between tribal and non-tribal society in the pre-British period, this relative isolation of the tribals definitely ended with colonialism. Once the British had consolidated their power in the sub-continent, they had little need for buffer states in the country, and as their colonial expansion began to open up even the more remote areas, the tribals were effectively brought under their rule.

This was no longer an acculturation from contact with a feudal society but an integration into "a colonial and capitalist matrix",[40] and it could not but have far-reaching and drastic effects on tribal society. As with other social groups the colonial administration —

> followed the dual policy of strengthening the feudal crust of the tribal societies, formed by the rajas, chiefs and zamindars and simultaneously created conditions in which their economy and political system were undermined by the rampaging market forces.[41]

Thus the tribal leadership was coopted into subservience to the British who actually enhanced their traditional hold over their local communities. More pertinently the tribal economy was progressively monetized and opened up to a host of money-lenders, traders, revenue farmers, etc.. And not unexpectedly, "these middlemen were the chief instruments of bringing the tribal people within the vortex of the colonial economy and exploitation".[42]

In attempting to reclaim these "primitives" for modern civilization, the colonial administration introduced private property rights in land which lead to a breakdown of the communal mode of production and control of common resources among these people. Processes of 'peasantization' and 'depeasantization' became inevitable, with the large scale transfer of land from tribals to non-tribals. Further the commercialization of the forests saw an alienation of traditional tribal rights in their familiar habitat.

The cumulative effect of all these changes was "the gradual disappearance of the non-market mechanisms of control of resources and allocation of goods, resulting in alienation, further bewilderment, poverty and confusion among tribals".[43] For their non-competitive, non-accumulative, egalitarian ethos was distinctly to their disadvantage now. In other words, the unequal exchange relation between the tribals and the outsiders deteriorated dramatically into an oppressive exploitation of the tribal community.

It is not surprising then that "the tribal people were among the earliest communities in India who fought against the British expansionism."[44] Stephen Fuchs makes an impressive catalogue of these tribal movements in his study of Rebellious Prophets.[45] Most of these movements though messianic and reformist in nature centered around, or were precipitated by issues concerning tribal lands and forests. However, their anti-colonialist perspective was not well articulated and they were unable to involve the non-tribal peasantry. They remained restricted and local and doomed to fail, when confronted by the power of the centralized, repressive, colonial state.

In places, a sympathetic and benevolent bureaucrat or a well-meaning missionary may have softened the blow. Moreover, some attempts at protective isolation for these tribals were made as early as the Scheduled Tracts of 1870 and the Scheduled Districts Acts of 1876, and later with the Backward Tracts of 1919, and the Excluded Areas and Partially Excluded Areas Act of 1936. But these were in actuality counter-productive and only led to greater, if perhaps more selective exploitation.

Certainly, the overall impact of the colonial period was to affect a profound and unenviable transformation of tribal dignity and identity in this country. This could be called the 'colonial mode of absorption' certainly more aggressive and penetrating than the earlier Hindu one. Of course, it would be the smaller and the less remote tribes who were the most vulnerable to these changes, as for instance the Kathkaris in western Maharastra.

The Post-independence Scene

With the end of the colonial rule there have been serious efforts made in the country to reverse this downward spiral and promote tribal welfare. Already the independence movement under Gandhi's leadership reacted sharply to the segregation of tribals and considered this to be part of the British colonial policy of divide and rule. Leaders like Rajendra Prasad in the north, and Thakkar Bapa in the west worked dedicatedly under Gandhian inspiration to uplift the tribals and bring them into the mainstream of national life.

In 1959 Nehru in his Foreword to Verrier Elwin's *Philosophy for NEFA*[46] set out the basis of the national policy on tribal development. This has remained its Magna Carta, its 'panchsheel' till today:

(a) People should be allowed to develop on the lines of their own genius and nothing should be imposed upon them,

(b) tribal rights on land and forests should be respected,

(c) induction of too many outsiders into tribal areas should be avoided,

(d) there should be no over administration of tribal areas as far as possible, and

(e) the results should not be judged by the amount of money spent but by the quality of the human character that is involved.

Unfortunately, in the hurly-burly of electoral politics, such noble ideals tend to be honoured more in the breech than in actuality. However, in this contemporary scene it is not just governmental policies and the implementation that need to be taken into account. Equally, if not more important are the tribal initiatives and responses, if indeed we consider them to be active subjects of their history and not abject sufferers of change.

The tribals have not been so isolated as to be the only actors in their history nor are any of these agents unaffected by the environment in which these interactions are situated. For human society is never mere puppet theatre, it is more like a tragic, oftentimes comic, sometimes even triumphant, but always a rich and complex drama. The 'script' for these actors may not be preset, but the stage on which their drama is enacted sets the parameters for the 'story line'. For the history of human freedom is always bounded by both physical and social necessity. However, it is the evolving patterns in this history that will yield the deepest significance of the drama. In responding to these creatively we can enhance our freedom and write our own story.

Evolutionary Patterns

Not all ethnologists would concede an evolving pattern in tribal society. For some "tribalism can be viewed as a reaction to the formation of a complex structure rather than a necessary preliminary stage in evolution".[47] They appear as primitive enclaves in juxtaposition to highly organised cultures. But this is a static, if not a reactionary view of tribal communities.

Other anthropologists have been more adept at enumerating stages in the development of the tribes, than in indicating the dynamics of their evolution. Thus L. P. Vidyarthi identifies six occupational groups among tribals today: hunters and food-gatherers, hill-cultivators, plains-farmers, simple artisans, cattle-keepers, and industrial-urban workers.[48] But these are more a descriptive than an analytical categorization.

Some scholars perceive the tribe as one of several stages, which,

> in the general evolution of society have been distinguished: (1) band, mainly confined to a hunting and food gathering society characterized by simple cooperation; (2) tribe referring to communities of settled fishing, simple horticulture or herding with limited exchanges between communities; (3) chiefdom related to more advanced horticulture or pastoralism with the beginnings of a social division of labour and institutionalized authority, and (4) state in which there are classes, monopoly force, and the centralized forceful mobilization of surplus product.[49]

However, the distinction between these categories are rather blurred and the original proposers of this schema, Sahlins and Service in 1960,[50] abandoned it later.

A century ago Marx and Engels writing about the "spontaneous community"[51] pointed to the endogenous causes for the breakdown of tribal society; the beginnings of private ownership within the communal mode of production, specially with the introduction of herding and luxury articles. Later Marxists have developed these insights in explaining the land-man relationship. Thus with hunters and food-gatherers, land is "the subject of labour", and we have communal ownership and an egalitarian band; where land is "the instrument of labour", we have private ownership and peasant society.[52]

More recently, from a Marxist perspective, M. Godelier has distinguished "between the two uses of the term tribe, seen as a type of society and as a stage of evolution", by emphasizing how "each stage of evolution is characterized by a specific mode of social organisation",[53] "as the mode of production changes the organisation of class in the evolution from tribe to chiefdom."[54] But this leaves out the question of multiple modes of production. Moreover, in considering a tribe to be a "completely organised society",[55] he seems to be assuming identifiable boundaries for tribal communities. But this is not very helpful in distinguishing tribal from non-tribal societies, especially in the context of tribal absorption in India.

An Ecological Approach

There have been many critiques of the Marxist model of analysis, which while acknowledging the insights it has yielded have also underlined its limitations. For

> whatever the merits of the mode of production concept while explaining differences in economic structure, this concept is of little use in explaining differences in the religious, cultural and ideological attributes of different societies.[56]

Hence an extension of "the mode of production", to "the concept of modes of resource use"[57] has been mooted, to include the availability of resources in the environment and the ecological impact of their use. This ecological perspective brings in a dimension that is particularly pertinent to those studying tribal societies, and specially relevant to the environmental crisis overtaking us all.

Gadgil and Guha, in their presentation of an ecological history of India, "from the long sweep of human history" find they "can distil four distinct modes of resource use: gathering (including shifting cultivation); nomadic pastoralism; settled cultivation; industry".[58] They give an elaborate comparison of the features of these four major models and their ecological impact.

In the evolution of human societies through these modes they identify five distinct but interrelated processes:

> First, there is an increasing intensity of resource use and exploitation. Second, there is a secular increase in the level of resource flows across different geographical regions and across different levels of any economic/political system. Third, there is an integration of larger and larger areas into the domain of any given political economic system. Fourth, there is, at the global level, a secular increase in population densities and in the extent of stratification and inequality

> with respect to the access, control and use of different natural resources. Finally, there is an intensification of rates of ecological change and ecological disturbance.[59]

At any given time, human societies will be at different stages along this evolutionary path, and they can enact their social drama only in the context of the historical processes and circumstances which set the stage for them. The better these are understood the more effect can the interventions of the actors be.

Conflict and Accommodation

Now where there is conflict within different modes of resource use in a particular society, there is often a struggle for control over resources that is "distorted to subserve the ends of a particular social group".[60] The 'circulation of elites' in a changing society is a convincing illustration of this. But when there is a conflict between modes of resource use "organised on very different social and ecological principles", especially when these are located in distinct social groupings this "has invariably resulted in massive outbursts of violent and sometimes genocidal conflict".[61] The clash of cultures between colonial and indigenous peoples all over the world are tragic evidence of this.

The stability of a group or community will depend on how effectively it occupies its ecological niche. And as these niches change with the adoption of new modes of resource use, it must effectively adapt and change if it is to survive and grow. For as old niches deteriorate or are closed, new ones must be generated or opened. Otherwise these communities will be forced into less and less viable niches where they will neither be able to sustain their cultural identity nor human dignity.

Of course a more effective mode of resource use only strengthens the resilience of a community *vis-a-vis* the other groups, and if this is sustainable use, then it will do to in relation to the environment as well. In this context the mode of resource use in tribal society may help them to leap-frog over the ecological crisis that threatens to destroy the urban-industrial societies which have precipitated it. But then again if the global environment itself is destroyed, the tribals may have no place to land but in the past!

The way our society accommodates the ecologically more balanced, though less immediately productive resource use of our tribals, is also a comment on, and a presage of the model of development what we as a nation chose for ourselves. For if we destroy the identity and dignity of our vulnerable tribals, what will we have not done to our own selves?

The tribals themselves are not just passive recipients in this process. All through their history we see them redefining and adapting their culture, resisting and rebelling against outside oppression. But the ecological niche they occupy today is extremely precarious, and they themselves very vulnerable, because of the changes in resource use and exploitation engulfing them. For as their environment degrades, so too does their society deteriorate. The post-independence period promised to reverse the damage of the colonial past. But it is a promise waiting to be fulfilled. Though for some of the smaller more exposed tribes it may be too late already.

CLARIFYING THE ISSUES

The colonial government's approach to the tribal welfare was mainly ameliorative, and intended to protect them from outside exploitation by isolating them, as in the "Excluded and Partially Excluded Areas Act" of 1936. Verrier Elwin in 1939 even suggested "the establishment of a sort of National Park" for tribals.[62] Such isolation, if possible in today's world, would amount to an enforced primitivism on tribal reservations, somewhat like the enforced captivity of animals in a zoo!

Government Initiatives

However, after independence the government's policies towards the tribals were no longer isolationist but designed to combine "the twin elements of protection and development. Seen in the perspective of the third world, the Indian Strategy of tribal development, in spite of its limitations, could be described as a unique experiment".[63]

Following Nehru's 'panchsheel', the idea now was not assimilation by either the Hindu or the colonial mode, but integration into the national mainstream, where their distinctive identity would not be lost, but would make its own unique contribution to the 'unity in diversity', that is India. However, as often happens in our "soft state" the gap between policy and performance is enormous.

By the sixth plan governmental agencies had set up a massive infrastructure to implement its programmes: 181 Integrated Tribal Development Agencies, 245 Marginal Areas Development Agencies, 73 projects for primitive communities, covering about 75 per cent of our tribal population.[64] Though these have made a real difference to the tribal situation in comparison to its pre-independence days, in relation to the other groups in our society today "they remain the most backward, underdeveloped and, next only to the scheduled castes, the most exploited community."[65]

Uneven Results

Moreover, the development achieved has been most uneven between and within tribes. Thus while some groups have made spectacular progress, others are still in the food-gathering and/or shifting cultivation stage. And even within the tribe, with protective discrimination and special facilities, a small elite has developed, "a creamy layer" as it is now called, with its own vested interests and the capacity to exploit their own less fortunate fellow tribals. This only stratifies a once egalitarian society into classes. All too often these tribal elites are coopted by other non-tribal ones, even at the cost of larger tribal interests for which they should have fought.

Now there would seem to be two main reasons for this failure of government policy other than inadequate or inconsistent implementation. The first is the very model of development adopted, i.e., a top-down one, that perpetuates unequal exchange relations between social groups and geographic areas, and marginalizes the poor and the powerless. The development debate in the last decade has resulted in an effective critique of this model, though planners and politicians are slow to abandon it because of their own vested interests perhaps. For the tribals the top-down interventions have been disastrous.

This brings us to the second reason for the failure of government policy with the tribals, which is more pertinent to our discussion here. Tribals have long been at a severe disadvantage when the outside world has intruded into their society, whether this was the colonial government or the national state. The clash of cultures that the development process introduces often leaves them worse off than before in many ways. They certainly do need protective discrimination to booster their capacity to absorb these developmental changes more effectively. But any paternalism, however benevolent, only serves to perpetuate further the unequal social relationships between tribals and non-tribals. So in spite of good intentions, the way is paved to an internal colonialism, that reproduces many of the most ugly features of the older, external one.

Tribal Responses

Stephen Fuchs distinguishes three responses of the tribals to their critical situation in developing India.[66] The one of rejection and regress into isolation will only leave them "practically condemned to total extinction".[67] Only a few of the nomadic forest tribes would opt for this. However, by far the largest portion are "ready to change their tribal ways of life and to go along with the national mainstream".[68] But they would not want to lose their tribal identity. What they do seem to want is integration, and not assimilation, as explained earlier. But there are also tribals who look "for another alternative, in the hope of saving their tribal identity and independence".[69] These are generally from among the larger, more geographically concentrated tribes. Some of these movements have even sought to secede from the Indian Union, as in the north-east, others have fought to express their solidarity in a tribal state within it, as the Jharkhand in Chotanagpur.

These movements are of course only the extreme expression of what many more tribes experience, though they are unable to mobilize themselves in response to it. For —

> one of the major roots of tribal solidarity movements may be traced to their ecological-cultural isolation, economic backwardness and a feeling of frustration about a lowly status vis-a-vis the advanced sections.[70]

What our tribals, then, seem to be looking for is an integration into our national society, which will respect their "cultural autonomy"[71] even as it gives them their economic and political place in the sun. Surely this is not an illegitimate or an unreasonable demand.

Understanding Development

The crux of the matter is the kind of development that our society is undergoing and how our tribals are to be integrated into, and not be assimilated by it. The development we strive to achieve must be distinguished by three characteristic features: an equity, that opposes all exploitation and inequality; a sustainability, that is ecologically sensitive to, and respectful of the environment; and a participation of the people in both, making the decisions that affect their lives and implementing them as well. Indeed, it is the people's participation at all levels that will be able to make the developmental process, equitable and sustainable as well.

Moreover, such an understanding of development makes possible the 'cultural autonomy', which will make all the difference between integration and assimilation for our tribals. Since tribes at various stages in their evolution will need different strategies tuned to their particular situation, only a genuine involvement of the people to be benefited by these strategies can bring an equitable and sustainable process of development.

Selective Incorporation

Now in the clash of cultures involved when differing modes of resource use come into competitive contact, one resolution to the conflict has been "the path of extermination,.... In this scenario, the earlier modes are more or less wiped out".[72] This has generally been the path of Europe, and its encounter with the non-European peoples.

> The alternative pattern, which we call the path of selective incorporation, better fits the history of the Indian sub-continent prior to its colonization by the British. In so far as the history of India exhibits the far greater overlap and coexistence of different modes of resource use, one can qualitatively distinguish the Indian experience from the European and the New World paradigm of eco-cultural change.[73]

Thus in the Indian experience,

> two complementary strategies, of leaving some ecological niches (hills, malarial forests) outside the purview of the peasant mode, and reserving certain niches within it for hunter-gatherers and pastorals, helped track a distinctive path of inter-modal cooperation and coexistence.[74]

Here the less resilient modes survived but were subordinated to the more dominant ones. In traditional Indian society such institutionalized hierarchy was acceptable to all groups. But as this changes, another more democratic basis for cooperation and coexistence must be found, unless we want to perpetuate "homo hierarchies", into the next millennium.

Today the clash of tribal and non-tribal cultures in our country is harsher and deeper because the changes our people are undergoing are more rapid and comprehensive than ever before. These —

> major and rapid social changes are associated with:

(a) loss of self-esteem;

(b) increase in actual and perceived role conflict and ambiguity;

(c) increase in the perceived gap between aspiration and achievement.[75]

The resulting anomie has precipitated reactionary and revivalist responses in many sections of our society. The aggressive fundamentalist religious movements sweeping our land today are evidence of this. Surely the tribals are the more vulnerable to rapid social change and so the more susceptible to a self-destructive anomie.

Efforts to mitigate and buffer the negative consequence of developmental change have certainly been made. "India is one of the few countries in the world with elaborate systems of preferential treatment for ascriptively defined groups,"[76] especially for the scheduled castes and tribes. But after almost half a century of independence, they still have a long way, to go to catch up with the mainstream, especially the smaller weaker tribes like the Kathkaris.

Fundamental Issues

The tribal question, therefore, raises fundamental issues for our society: of social equity, ecological sustainability, and peoples' participation; of cultural autonomy and democratic integration. For "the tribal problem cannot be isolated from the broader national problems. Its solution will have to form part of the overall strategy for the regeneration of Indian society and polity".[77]

For in India national development cannot be separated from tribal integration, or for that matter from the marginalized minorities in our society. Our own future is more closely bound up with theirs than we perhaps realize. For in Ashish Nandy's paraphrase of

> the ancient wisdom implied in the New Testament and also perhaps in the Sauptik Parva of the *Mahabharata:* 'Do not do unto others what you would that they do not unto you, lest you do unto yourself what you do unto others' [78]

REFERENCES

1. Andre Gunder Frank, *Development of Underdevelopment*, Monthly Review Press, New York, 1969.
2. Ref. S.G. Deogaonkar, *Tribal Development Plans: Implementation and Evaluation*, Concept Pub., New Delhi, 1992, p. 14.
3. *Pocket Oxford Dictionary*, Oxford University Press, London, 1934, p. 898.

4. I. M. Lewis, "Tribal Society", in David L. Sills, ed., *International Encyclopedia of the Social Sciences,* Vols.15, 16, 17, p. 146 (pp. 146-150).
5. *ibid.*
6. Charles Winick, *Dictionary of Anthropology,* Peter Owen, London, 1960, p.546.
7. Jaganath Pathy, *Tribal Peasantry: Dynamics of Development,* Inter-India Publication, New Delhi, 1984, p. 2.
8. Ref. Nirmal Sengupta, 'Reappraising Tribal Movements'--II, *Economic and Political Weekly,* Vol. 23, No. 20, 14 May 1988, p. 1003.
9. Stephen Fuchs, *The Aboriginal Tribes of India,* Macmillan India, Delhi, 1974, p. 24.
10. *Report of the Commissioner for Scheduled Castes and Tribes,* Government of India, New Delhi, 1952, p. 77.
11. Ref. T. B. Naik, 'What is a Tribe? Conflicting Definitions', in *Applied Anthropology,* ed., L. P. Vidyarthi, Kitab Mahal, Allahabad, 1968, pp. 84-97.
12. Piarey Lal Metha, *Constitutional Protection to Scheduled Tribes in India: Retrospect and Prospect,* H. K. Publishers and Distributors, Delhi, 1991, p. 27.
13. Cf. J. Pathy, *op. cit.,* p.6.
14. Cf. Andre Beteille, *Society and Politics in India,* Oxford Univ. Press, Delhi, 1992, Ch. 3, 'The Concept of Tribe with Special Reference to India', pp. 57-78, Cf. also Beteille, *Essays in Comparative Sociology,* Oxford Univ. Press, Delhi, 1987, Ch.4, Appendix, "On the Concept of Tribe", pp. 77-81, and "The Definition of a Tribe", in Romesh Thaper, ed., *Tribe, Caste and Religion in India,* Macmillan, Delhi, 1977, pp.12-14.
15. P. L. Metha, *op. cit.,* p. 57.
16. *Report of the Commissioner, op. cit.* p. 9.
17. Buddhadeb Chaudhuri, editor, *Tribal Transformation in India, Inter-India Publication,* New Delhi, 1992, Vol. I, Preface, p. viii.
18. Jaganath Pathy, *Ethnic Minorities in the Process of Development,* Rawat Publications, Jaipur, 1988, p.25.
19. *ibid.* p.20.
20. *ibid.* p.22.
21. Jawaharlal Handoo, "Far From Truth: Anthropology and Tribal Studies", in Buddhadeb Chaudhuri, ed., *Tribal Transformation in India,* Vol.III, *op. cit.,* p. 39 (pp.35-42).
22. Cf. S. C. Dube, "Approaches to the Tribal Problem in India", in L. P. Vidyarthi, ed., *op.cit.,* pp.107-112.
23. J. Handoo, *op. cit., ibid.*
24. S. L. Doshi, *Tribal Ethnicity, Class and Integration,* Rawat Pub., Jaipur, 1990, p. 70.
25. J. Pathy, *Tribal Peasantry, op. cit.,* p. 26.
26. J. Forsyth, *The Highlands of Central India,* Chapman and Hall, London, 1889, p. 17.
27. G. S. Ghurye, *The Scheduled Tribes,* Popular Press, Bombay, 1963, p. 19.
28. *ibid.,* p. 56.
29. N. K. Bose, *Culture and Society in India,* Asia Pub. House, Bombay, 1967, pp. 213-15.
30. D. D. Kosambi, *The Culture and Civilization of Ancient India in Historical Outline,* Routledge and Kegan Paul, London, 1965, p.172.
31. Suniti Kumar Chatterji, *The Indo-Mongoloids: Their Contributions to the History and Culture of India,* Royal Asiatic Society of Bengal, Calcutta, 1951.
32. *Religion and Society Among the Coorges of South India,* Asia Pub. House, Bombay, 1952.
33. J. Pathy, *Ethnic Minorities, op. cit.,* p.157.
34. D. G. Mandelbam, *Society in India,* Popular Prakashan, Bombay, 1970, p. 593.
35. A. R. Desai, "Tribes in transition", in Buddhadeb Chaudhuri, ed., *Tribal Development in India, op. cit.,* p. 514 (pp.505-18).

36. D. D. Kosambi, *An Introduction to the Study of Indian History*, Popular Prakashan, Bombay, 1975, p. 49.
37. B. K. Roy Burman, "Persistence of Folk Law in India with Particular Reference to Tribal Communities", in *Tribal Transformation in India, op. cit.*, Vol. III, p.174, pp. 173-87.
38. *ibid.*
39. *ibid.* p. 177.
40. A. R. Desai, *op. cit.*, p. 515.
41. K. S. Singh, *Tribal Society in India: An Anthropo-Historical Perspective*, Manohar, New Delhi, 1985, p. 248.
42. Bipan Chandra, et. al., *India's Struggle for Independence, 1857-1947*, Viking, New Delhi, 1988, p. 45.
43. Ajit K. Danda, "Economic Transformation of Tribals in India", in Buddhadeb Chaudhuri, ed., *Tribal Development in India, op. cit.*, p. 502 (pp. 495-504).
44. J. Pathy, *Tribal Peasantry, op. cit.*, p. 66.
45. Stephen Fuchs, *Rebellious Prophets: A Study of Messianic Movements in Indian Religious*, Asia Pub. House, Bombay, 1965.
46. Verrier Elwin, *Philosophy for NEFA* (2nd ed.), Govt. of Assam, Shillong, 1959.
47. Morton Fried, "On the Concepts of Tribe and Tribal Society", in June Helm, *ed.*, *Essays on the Problem of Tribe*, Proceedings of the 1967 Annual Spring Meeting of the American Ethnological Society, Seattle, 1968, p. 15 (pp. 3-20).
48. Cf. L. P. Vidyarthi, "Strategy for Tribal Development in India", Proceedings of the Seminar on Tribal Development, Bhubaneshwar, 1975.
49. J. Pathy, *Tribal Peasantry, op. cit., pp.* 8-9.
50. Marshall D. Sahlins and E. R. Service, *Evolution and Culture*, University of Michigan Press, Ann Arbor, 1960, pp. 36-7.
51. Karl Marx and F. Engels, *Pre-Capitalist Socio-Economic Formations*, Progress Pub., Moscow, 1979.
52. Claude Meillassous, "From Reproduction to Production: A Marxist Approach to Economic Anthropology", *Economy and Society*, Vol. I, No. I, 1972, pp. 93-105.
53. M. Godelier, *Perspectives in Marxist Anthropology*, Cambridge Univ. Press, London, 1977, p.70.
54. *ibid.* p.87.
55. *ibid.*
56. Madhav Gadgil and Ramachandra Guha, *This Fissured Land: An Ecological History of India*, Oxford University Press, Delhi, 1992, p.12.
57. *ibid.* p.13.
58. *ibid.* p. 14.
59. *ibid.* p. 64.
60. *ibid.* p. 57.
61. *ibid.* p. 53.
62. Verrier Elwin, *The Baiga*, John Murray, London, 1939, pp. 511-19.
63. K. S. Singh, *Tribal Society, op. cit.*, p. 250.
64. Cf. B. K. Burman Roy, "Issues in Tribal Development", in B. Chaudhuri, *ed.*, *Tribal Transformation in India, op. cit.*, Vol. II, p.11 (pp. 3-20).
65. K. S. Singh, *Tribal Society, op. cit.*, p. 254.
66. Stephen Fuchs, "The Religion of Indian Tribals", in B. Chaudhuri, ed., *Tribal Transformation in India, op. cit.*, Vol. V, p. 50 (pp. 23-51).
67. *ibid.*
68. *ibid.*
69. *ibid.*
70. Surajit Sinha, "Tribal Solidarity Movements in India", in B. Chaudhuri, *ed.*, *Tribal*

Development, op. cit., p. 177 (pp. 163-79).

71. Robert Goodland, *Tribal Peoples and Economic Development; Human Ecologic Considerations*, World Bank, Washington, 1982, p.28.
72. Gadgil and Guha, *op. cit.*, p.109.
73. *ibid.*
74. *ibid.* p. 110.
75. Robert Goodland, *op. cit.*, p. 25.
76. J. Pathy, *Tribal Peasantry, op. cit.*, p. 163.
77. S. C. Dube, "Inaugural Address", in K.S. Singh, ed., *The Tribal Situation in India*, Indian Institute of Advanced Study, Shimla, 1972, p.32.
78. Ashish Nandy, *The Intimate Enemy: Loss and Recovery of Self Under Colonialism*, Oxford University Press, Delhi, 1983, p. 31.

2
METHODOLOGICAL DILEMMAS AND DIFFICULTIES

INTRODUCTION

The review of the historical evolution of the tribals in this country serves to make us acutely aware of how the prejudgments and presuppositions of those who studied them, have affected our perceptions of these people. Here we will attempt to design a methodology that will not repeat the short-comings of the past, and hopefully avoid falling into new pitfalls as well. For this we must steer our way carefully between the horns of some daunting dilemmas.

Subjects and Objects

Referring to its birth during western colonialism, Levi-Strauss writes: "anthropology is daughter to this era of violence" for it "reflects on the epistemological level, a state of affairs, in which one part of mankind treated the other as an object".[1] Thus the dominance-subservience relationship of the colonizer and the colonized was reproduced in the anthropological discourse, and with the end of colonialism still carried on by local non-tribals studying the tribals, once again reflecting the same unequal relationships. Certainly, no real empathetic understanding can come from this.

Obviously if the people being studied are not to be treated as 'objects' then some space must be made in the discourse for their subjectivity. Indeed, if no social science can exclude the subjectivity of the scientist himself, it would hardly make for a more 'objective science' to exclude the subjectivity of the people being studied. Rather it would only allow more fair play for the subjectivity of the researcher. And this is a better guarantee of a more authentic comprehension.

Alien Observers and Indigenous Participants

The social sciences have by now shaken off the methodological hegemony of the natural sciences that they aped for a while. The subjectivity-objectivity debate has been resolved in a realistic and practical dialectic between the two. The same must now be done with, what Marvin Harris called, the 'etic', or the observer's point of view, and the 'emic' or the participant's viewpoint.[2]

Now among the social scientists in the third world, their etic perceptions are often dominated by the concepts and categories of the west which are often alien to their intellectual tradition and situation. But then again "the local ways of conceptualizing objects and categories in their existence and dynamics are not necessarily comprehensive or superior".[3] For these too can reflect the local dominant-dependent relationships of an internal rather than an external colonialism, even though these may perhaps be more tradition-based. And so this may end up "studying tribal cultures in India the way the western anthropologists studied us-city-bred Indians".[4]

Moreover, a more universal perspective has a very positive value in opening a window on to a wider scenario, which at times could in fact help to ground a more particular approach as well. Reciprocally this could also happen when first world researchers turn to their own societies after a third world experience, unless one holds with Kipling that "East is East and West is West and n'er the twain shall meet". Here too, the need is to hold the two perspectives in creative tension.

Micro and Macro Approaches

When the case study method is applied to a "little community",[5] there is the danger of a microscopic examination becoming myopic. In the depth of detail, the breadth of vision can be lost. But the details need not be described as fragments, but perceived as adding up to a 'whole', which is "microcosmic--capable of reflecting worlds larger than themselves".[6] In other words, one, which can in miniature be a representation of the larger macrocosm. An analogy to the hologram in laser optics would illustrate this rather well.

But there is another aspect to this micro- macro dilemma. Robert Redfield speaks of a "worm's eye view", i.e., the examination or study of "the effect of a great movement on a remote people".[7] Here it is the micro-study that contextualizes and concertizes macro-processes. And when this is a view from the 'underside', from the subalterns in society, it becomes an invaluable, if not a necessary, complement to a more comprehensive understanding of these macro-process themselves. This of course does not belittle the importance or value of a 'bird's eye view', rather it makes it in turn a necessary complement as well.

Procedure and Intuition

But beyond these necessarily complementary and critically essential points of view there is also the question of methodological procedure. One way of proceeding is to cautiously accumulate certified data and wait until it adds up to a planned illumination of a well defined space. Another way is to sketch in bold lines the alternative interpretations that the data may suggest, though these are still more persuasively tentative, than definitively conclusive.

In the first instance we use the data more analytically to set up a test, or 'null' hypothesis which we then try to falsify by an experimental or statistical test. In this procedure of falsification our concern is to reject, or not to accept, an hypothesis that is in fact false. In the second instance we use the data more exploratively and intuitively to generate alternative hypotheses and accumulate data to verify them. In this procedure of verification our concern is not to, reject, but accept an hypothesis, that is in fact true.

Positivist science generally uses the falsification procedure because it is more rigorous, especially when used with objectified, quantitative data. However, an interpretative discipline is better suited to the less rigorous procedure of verification, especially since the data is qualitative and more subjective. It is here that breakthroughs to alternative explanatory models are often made.

Once again these two procedures do not negate each other, and both must be part of an enduring scientific endeavour. One must indeed be sure that the pieces identified belong to the original jigsaw puzzle, or it will never be put together. But one does not have to have the very last piece certified before one can begin to grasp the overarching pattern. It takes an imaginative leap to comprehend the whole picture. The greater the leap the greater the corresponding risk of missing the real pattern, or even falsifying the true picture. But then again even giant leaps must often be preceded by many small steps. In other words, while being sensitive to the need for a 'fine-tuned methodology' we must not let a 'tyranny of methodology' render pertinent data invisible, or bold conceptualizations unacceptable, and so obstruct rather than facilitate more insightful interpretations and more empathetic understandings.

Steps and Leaps

The scope of this study is too modest to be placed anywhere but among those small steps, however, we hope it is a firm, if small step towards some giant's leap!

For this the design and execution of this study will attempt to hold in a creative dialectic tension the apparent contradictions we have just explained, between the subjective and the objective, the etic and the emic, the western and the Indian, the universal and the particular, the micro and the macro, a worm's eye view and a bird's eye view, the small procedural step and the giant imaginative leap. No doubt a difficult but surely a challenging and promising task.

Participatory Action Research

A conventional research methodology would hardly be adequate to this challenge. For one, it distances the researcher from any action-involvement in the field supposedly for the sake of scientific objectivity. Moreover, it legitimizes the alienation of precisely those participants in the study who are crucial for any balance of the methodological preoccupations of these academic researchers with the real life concerns of people in the field. Hence for the purposes of this study a participatory action research was far more relevant and meaningful.[8]

For if a researcher comes to the field with already full blown theoretical hypotheses and sharply defined analytical concepts, this may lend intellectual sophistication to the study, however, it cannot but make any subaltern point of view and understanding tangential to the study, if it does not leave it out completely. And yet even committed activists can become ideologically petrified, forcing facts to fit their prejudices. Neither of these allow for more meaningful interpretations, that might be outside their frame of reference, to question their assumptions or conclusions.

For this the active participation of the various constituents in this research-action procedure is called for at three levels: investigation, analyses and follow up. But this is more the ideal than the reality. There are both, difficulties intrinsic to the process of participation itself, such as differing levels of comprehension and commitment, of the participants, as well as the extrinsic constraints of time and expense in organising and coordinating this complex process.

Yet authentic collaborative and non-manipulative relationships are essential to any participatory procedure, which must avoid the skewed asymmetry of a dominant dependent exchange. Rather it must be characterized by an open and respectful encounter between as many of the constituencies as possible. However, the direct participation of all the various constituents in the process, remains an unattainable ideal. It must be realistically compromised at times, or at others mediated through various spokespersons and leaders. Participants must meet at the level at which they are, for only then can they move progressively to broaden and intensify the participatory base of this process. However, unreconciled dilemmas, and unspecified agendas, will remain.

Now if we are looking for an on-going praxis of action and research, then, "involvement above all may be essential for going ahead with the research itself. Participation may become a source of data and insight....Purists in research methodology may be outraged at such contaminations of the field of action, but the pragmatic fieldworker cannot shy away from involvement when it can lead to insight. Methodological purism can be sterile".[9]

Rather obviously, then, an action oriented research will be more concerned with the process oriented conscientization of people, than the product-directed results of academics. And yet it is necessary to steer between the ad hoc empiricism of the activists and the ungrounded theory of the researchers. Further the participatory approach is complementary and compatible with bottom up strategies, whether this be in research or development.

THE STUDY DESIGN

This study was planned as an action-oriented participative research and not merely as an academic exercise. As such a neat preciseness in design and execution were less important than carrying along all those collaborating on it. It was meant to deepen the understanding of those in the field and also the ones they worked with.

There were thus three groups of persons collaborating in this study. The researchers, the social workers and the people. But as may be expected, the levels of understanding and participation in the study design, would broadly correspond to the levels of involvement and commitment to its field execution. But then again the wider usefulness of this study can indeed extend beyond the immediate participants, to other similar situations.

The Purpose

This study is intended to address some of the more crucial issues regarding tribal minorities in this country. The earlier chapter was devoted precisely to a discussion of such issues. In this context then the questions specifically posed here will concern the changing ethnic identity and deteriorating minority status of these tribals, with the purpose of facilitating a deeper, more empathetic understanding and evolving an action-reflection process in an on-going praxis.

Within this overall purpose, the objectives of the study can be articulated thus:

1. reconstructing the Kathkari profile from a critical examination of the available sources;
2. analysing the perceptions of Kathkari identity and dignity from the field-data collected; and
3. drawing out the wider implications for similarly placed groups from the significant findings here.

Beginning then with group discussion of documentary sources available, the study included a collaborative collection of field-data, and a collective reflection, analysis and feedback. The monograph here is but the outcome of this participative process.

Data Collection Instruments

The interview schedules focussed on the respondents perception of the Kathkaris and their changing situation. It was administered to three sets of persons in the field: the non-tribals, the social workers and the Kathkaris themselves. Since the participatory method allows for a variety of approaches to data-collection and analysis, here too, besides indepth interviews with individuals, group discussions, community meetings, participative action programmes, etc., were all sources of information and collective reflection.

The schedule itself provided the main themes for discussion and reflection, formulated in two parts. The first, on the changing identity covering topics like occupation, status, kinship, etc; the second, on their declining dignity, including aspects and agents of change. The schedule was introduced differently to each group of respondents and pragmatically adapted to get the best out of sometimes difficult and trying situations in the field. The interview and discussion schedules are reproduced in the appendix, to this chapter.

Further data on the Kathkari settlements involved, was collected on village-level characteristics; demographic, economic, socio-religious, political, etc.. This forms an important background for a more contextualized interpretation and analysis. Part of this village-level data is presented in the appendix below.

THE FIELDWORK

Participative Interaction

In conformity with our theoretical perspective and the

methodological approach outlined we wanted to carry out the entire endeavor in a manner which did not view the community as an isolated unit. We interacted with those Kathkari settlements which were in touch with the social workers of the Janahit Vikas Trust and were involved in its various programmes. While the trust was working largely with this community, it was also involved with villages of other ethnic groups. As part of our investigations included the attitudes of non-Kathkaris towards the tribe, inter-acting with these groups was also relevant to the project. The social workers themselves were an important resource as they play a complementary role in making political choices which affect the community.

While interaction with the Kathkaris began in the month of August 1992, we were already making notes and identifying sources from early January the same year, as the programs of the Janahit Vikas Trust for the following year were being chalked out and earlier plans reviewed. In each statement of the social workers discussing the successes and failures of their programmes, was embodied a particular vision of the Kathkaris. Their statements arose from an intimate contact with the community and all their frustrations and triumphs were partially indicative of the cultural and political future of the community. But like some of their predecessors, many of them reflected the same negative stereotypes about the Kathkaris which influenced their actual interaction.

The dominant communities of the area, mainly the landed population, include the Marathas and Agris. These utilize Kathkari labour on an everyday basis which shapes their attitude towards these tribals in specific ways. The areas which are industrialized, have an urbanized population living very close to the traditional habitats of the tribe. Not surprisingly it is mostly the outsiders and newcomers to the area that have cornered most of the benefits of change, a development in which the tribals have only the lowest position, if any at all.

Interaction with both these groups gave insights into the cultural and economic changes taking place in the region. The official government statements made during a seminar, conversations on buses and tea shops, the experiences of other social work organizations, especially the Yusuf Meherally Centre (YMC), which was started in May 1961, and had inaugurated a clinic in Tara village in 1967, and has been involved with the adivasis of the area since then,[10] all these were important sources for our 'data' to understand the complexities of a changing tribal identity in a rapidly industrializing district.

An Open-ended Approach

In such a context, the fieldwork done amongst the Kathkari community could not consist of simple question-answer sessions. Observations of the habitat, inquiries seemingly unrelated to the actual questionnaire, counter-checks made by questioning neighbouring groups were all on-the-spot improvizations of our formal plan. The statements made by the respondents could not be decontextualized from specific political and cultural processes affecting their localities, as these were bound to be influential. Making generalized statements was something we avoided as much as possible, even as the emerging picture may have shown some common elements.

The eleven Kathkari settlements we visited, were all participating in the programmes organized by the Janahit Vikas Trust. The social workers were the link in our interaction, as they were familiar and trusted faces. Before our visits we would get some idea about the economic and political state of each settlement and note their experiences with the inhabitants. The 'naik' was usually the first member with whom we would communicate and then he would introduce us to the others. But much of our information was given by the naik himself, and we did not see him as distorting the supposedly more 'real' discourse of the other folk. He is rarely in an economically better position than the others and only voices their views. In fact, the common economic lifestyle of most inhabitants, as they are still in a state of collective deprivation, lends a certain uniformity to their responses. This of course, does not justify us idealizing their "strong community ties" or oversimplifying their statements by glossing over individual differences.

As our inquiries were related to questions of political and economic choices, which were bound to be common responsibilities considering their present economic condition, the relative uniformity of responses reveals a more or less well accepted course of action or stand. Here it is not only the naik who plays an important role but also other political agencies like parties or activist organizations which complement their political perceptions, often insinuating their own interests into the process.

But there were notable exceptions. We did find the youth often differing on the questions of political choices, feeling that they were in a more advantageous position to make the correct one. But by and large differences were not so acute that they could be treated separately. Thus we discovered a settlement that had broken off from another one, following a fight between the "naik" and his son, but this difference did not translate itself into any major divergent political stand.

Practical Limitations

One limitation we had was that most of our individual interaction happened to be with men. But this was, hopefully, balanced by the fact that nearly all the social workers, especially the many women among them, had fairly good relationships with the women of the settlements. So through their experiences, we would get a fairly even representation in our study. However, in quite a few discussion sessions, women participants were as active as men . Our own observations too, regarding the kind of work being done by the two sexes, or their attitudes towards gender relations would be a more direct complement to the statements made by the respondents.

The presence of social workers during our meetings had an additional advantage. Many of our discussions would centre on arguments between the members of the community and the social workers, regarding the construction of a school or the digging of a well, bringing to the surface aspects of their life which would have remained latent otherwise. Our procedure for data-collection was not the kind of conventional fieldwork done by anthropologists, which requires a long period of residence in the village, getting detailed information and insights into their everyday life. Nor did it include a closed-ended and quantitative questionnaire. Rather it was a participative approach mediated by an agency familiar with the people. This, was an important advantage to our mind.

The entire endeavor was carried out keeping in mind the specific demands made by our project. We were aware that the study would not be able to fully grasp the complexities of the people, their beliefs and needs, in a rapidly changing environment, and that the information and insights gained would not be representative of the entire community. The very fact that each locality would nuance the story of its respondents in its own a peculiar way, made us resist simplified generalizations. Revisiting a settlement after as brief a period as one month, would often elicit a different response, probably influenced by some local event. The social workers would tell us stories about the settlement which often contradicted the records based on our own discussions with the members. All these complexities make for a tentative understanding, not a definitive one.

At the same time our study will show that the problems faced by the community are not so incomprehensible that political choices become impossible for these people. If anything at all, the community views its situation with a critical eye and is not unaware of the combination of group interests and historical processes, responsible for their present situation. On the other hand we also came across severe self-criticism often bordering on self-depreciation, reinforced by their interaction with other groups on whom they were dependent.

With other communities, it was not very difficult to get their views on the Kathkaris. These settlements were also familiar with the social workers and the inhabitants were spontaneous in their responses, ready to enter into discussion and debate over issues varying from dowry to politics, and were more than willing to talk about the Kathkaris. These views differed from community to community reflecting their own particular relationship with the tribe.

Time-frame

This study was begun in 1992 and completed in 1993. The field work was done mostly in the latter half of 1992 and the first part of 1993. The findings were presented to and discussed by the Janahit Vikas team before being written in its final form in this monograph.

CONCLUSION

In describing the fieldwork for this study some of the limitations encountered in executing the research design no doubt become apparent. At the same time some of the more fortuitous circumstances also come to light. Though not all these limiting encounters or lucky circumstances can be recorded here, hopefully they all add up to a picture of more light than shadow.

The dialectical opposition between the methodological polarities explained at the beginning of this chapter, represent both a challenge and a risk: holding them in creative tension or falling between both poles. Practical constraints might indicate prudential decisions, which might appear as compromising to some or facilitating to others, depending on how critically demanding we want to be. Not all such decisions in the field can be anticipated, indeed many of them are more implicitly made, than explicitly discussed. It is only in retrospect that we can know how successfully we have met the challenge and not lost out on the risks taken.

Particularly problematic in a participative study like this, is the balance between the subjective and the objective, the insider's emic point of view and the outsider's etic one. For it easily tilts in favour of the more active participants, in this case the researchers and social workers. But these are still outsiders for the people, who remain the subjects of the study. And yet involving the people more actively entails opportunity costs, which they may justifiably be unwilling to accept.

Again, with regard to indigenous or alien conceptual categories, avoiding the 'alien' leaves us with no adequate 'indigenous' framework as yet. For those, who have studied Indian tribals have drawn lean heavily from the western and rather meagerly from the tribal conceptual world. Hence it would seem best to start with the framework we have, to build the framework we want, knowing that we run the unavoidable risk of being trapped where we began not breaking free to where we want to be. In this study, we can only claim to have begun with a small step in the right direction.

Finally, our focusing on Kathkari identity and dignity represents an emphasis on the particular, the micro, which we then try to set in the more universal, the more macro context of ethnicity and minority status. Here it is possible that the worm's eye view and the bird's eye view may end up describing parallel or contradictory entities. But if the perspectives turn out to be converging and complementary, then it could make for a giant leap forward. This study does not claim as much, but only that it strives to be more than just a faltering dwarfed step.

The earlier chapter set the larger and more general context for the tribal question. The next two will consider the more particular and specific situation of the Kathkari tribals.

APPPENDIX I.

THE INTERVIEW/DISCUSSION SCHEDULE

Identity and Dignity : The Changing Profile of the Kathkaris.

Note

The following is a loose and open-ended technical aid for data-collection. More than a questionnaire, it is a guide for an unstructured interview or discussion with the respondents. Conversations can be steered in the direction as shown by the schedule, but at the same time it leaves enough space for spontaneous diversions. It is also an important guide to keep one from being totally disorganized and unstructured in the collection of data. Hence the detailed divisions and sub-divisions in the organization of the questions, for collecting information in accordance with each sub-topic. They do not have to be followed in the same order as given. Their main function is to keep one from making omissions and loosing track of our concerns. Time limits are not stated and can be made flexible according to context, keeping in mind the eliciting of the best kind of information. The involvement with the people on the part of the data-collector will be the most important variable in the quality of information gathered and observations recorded.

PART I

A Survey of the Self-perception of Kathkaris

Introduction

Every human culture develops an identity, distinguishing it from other groups, even as each of them may be interdependent. Interdependence implies exchange, both material as well as symbolic, which in turn signifies the existence of distinguishable characteristics in every group.

This is why every human culture develops its own identity, positive or, as may happen in certain circumstances, negative at times. However, if no culture lacks an identity, many groups are forced to live without dignity, a factor directly related to economic, political and cultural inequalities. It is here that we have to make a distinction between both these concepts.

The Kathkaris are experiencing a changing identity, but how has this affected their sense of dignity and pride?

I. Identity

Introduction

Who is a Kathkari?

Occupation/Work.

What work do most Kathkaris do?
What is your main occupation?
How much do you earn everyday?
Is it enough for you/your family?
What did the Kathkaris do in the past?
What was your parents main occupation?
How does it differ from yours?
Did your parents' occupation provide them their requirements?
What work would you like your children to do on growing up?
What is the best kind of work you would like for yourself, for your children?
What are the possessions you would like to have most?

Status/Caste

Which are the other jatis you interact with?
How do you interact with them? Friendly, hostile?
Which of them are your superiors? And which your inferiors? What exactly do you do for them and what do they do for you, in terms of services rendered?
Who benefits whom and how?
How do the other jatis treat you?
In what way do you differ from each of them?
What are the positive features of your jati you would like to keep?
And the negative features you would like to change?

Family/Kinship

Are you married?
If yes, who chose your marriage partner?
If not, who will choose your marriage partner?
From where does the marriage partner usually come from?
Which are the different clans in your village?

Was there any monetary exchange during the marriage? If yes, then of what kind?
What work do each of you do, both, husband and wife?
Is there anything which one spouse does, and the other is prohibited from doing?
Do any of you desire a child of a particular sex? Why or why not?
Which is the most respected family in your settlement?
What are the special powers which the headman, the 'naik', has?
How does one become the 'naik' of the village?

Religion.

Which religious festivals do you celebrate?
What are the major rites of birth, naming, puberty, marriage and death?
Which gods and goddesses are worshipped in your family?
What is the god of your clan/village?
Do you fast? When and why?
Is there any atma in trees and stones? Are they good or evil? Or both?
Do you employ the services of a priest? What do they do?
Have you gone to a bhagat? When and why?
Where do you go when you are sick?
Do you go to a doctor? Why do you prefer going to a bhagat? (or doctor, in context of the response)

II. Dignity

Aspects for change

Which jati do you think has progressed most and why?
What are the negative features of the Kathkaris you want to do away with or change?
What do you feel are your positive features?
Are you respected by other jatis in your present occupation? What else would you like to do?
What job would you like your children to have which would give them due respect?

Agents for change

Are you literate? If yes, upto what level?
Would you like to learn?
If no, why not?

What are the advantages/disadvantages of literacy, *vis-a-vis* economic betterment?
What are the immediate sacrifices you have to make to become literate? Or to send your child to a school?
How important is money for enhancing dignity?
Does education enhance your awareness? How?
Does the government ever help you in improving your lifestyle? (regarding income, etc.).
What are your expectations from the government?
What are your expectations from the social workers, voluntary agencies and non-government organizations?
Would you like your child to be educated? Why?

Note

Parts II and III of the schedule covered much the same ground as Part I. Here only the pertinent differences are given.)

Part II A Survey of the Awareness and Attitudes of the Social Worker about the Kathkaris.

Introduction

Social change of any kind is facilitated by the interaction and intervention of various groups, and often these are intentional. It is difficult to talk of a pure Kathkari identity as if various historical factors have never touched them. The British banning of liquor manufacture by the Kathkaris and the consequent integration of them into the market economy is as much a part of Kathkari history as is their traditional occupation of Katechu making, which gave these people their name, a thing of the past.

Social workers, as an intervening group are non-exploitative, and the exchange relation they share with the Kathkaris, acts in their favour besides being an important aid in helping them cope with changing identities and lifestyles.

1. Name.
2. Age.
3. Sex.
4. Duration of contact with the Kathkaris.
5. Aspects of change.

What are the positive/negative features of the Kathkaris which you feel promotes/negates the processes of their economic betterment.

What kind of work are the Kathkaris best suited for?

Do you feel that there has been a decline in their pride with changing occupations, in the eyes of other jatis?

What can be done to restore their pride and dignity?

Agents of change

Do you feel that education can play an important role in their betterment? In what way?

What is the level of literacy in your area?

Do you find the Kathkaris eager to learn?

If not, what could be the reason?

If yes, what do you feel has made the Kathkaris look at literacy in a positive manner?

In what concrete ways do you feel education can help them?

Besides reading and writing, what else would be of interest and use to the Kathkaris?

What according to you can the government, voluntary organizations and NGOs do to help the Kathkaris? What expectations do the Kathkaris have, with the above mentioned organizations and how do they interact with them?

What are the main obstacles you as a social worker, and your organization face as you interact with the Kathkaris?

Part III A Survey of the Non-Kathkari Perception of the Kathkari Tribals.

Introduction

An identity is never formed in isolation but through constant interaction with other cultural groups. This is especially true of the Kathkaris who have always had relations with other tribal and non-tribal communities in the neighbourhood. The relations were both, economic as well as cultural.

Besides identity, dignity is another factor which is directly related to the perception of other groups, especially when the interaction is between a caste and a non-caste society.

Notions of superiority, as well as economic inequalities are directly linked to the question of dignity among the Kathkaris *vis-a-vis* other communities in the area.

Identity

What is the name of your jati?
What is your occupation?
Who are the Kathkaris?
Do you interact with them?
What is the kind of relationship you share with them? Is it friendly or hostile?
Do you feel that they should be satisfied with their present condition of living?
If not, then whom do you hold responsible for their state?
What kind of occupation do you think that they are best suited for?

Status/Caste.

Are the Kathkaris your superiors or inferiors?
What role does your jati perform for them?
What role do they perform for you?
Do you eat and drink with them?
Does your community intermarry with them?
Do you feel that the Kathkaris had a different relation with you in the past? In what way has it changed?
In what way do you consider yourself different from the Kathkaris?
In what way are you similar?
With respect to other jatis in the neighborhood, where would you place the Kathkaris?
Do you feel that the Kathkaris will change with the times?

APPENDIX II

THE VILLAGES IN THE STUDY

Name and location of villages in the study

All the villages are in Raigad District in Western Maharashtra.

1. *Pui,* 1 km. off the Bombay-Goa highway at Kolhad village, about 60 kms. from Panvel, Roha taluka.
2. *Shedashi,* 15 kms from Pen on the Khopoli road, and 2 kms off this road, Pen taluka.
3. *Bhuneshwar,* 2 kms off the Roha-Kolad road, Roha taluka.
4. *Khairatwadi,* 14 kms from Panvel on the Goa road, Panvel taluka.
5. *Berle,* 8 kms from Panvel on the Panvel-Pune highway, 2 kms off this highway, Panvel taluka.
6. *Killa,* 4 kms from Roha on the Kolhad road, 2 kms off this road, Roha taluka.
7. *Barsoli,* 2 kms east from Roha town, Roha taluka.
8. *Palekhurd,* 1 km beyond the Kathkariwadi at Killa, Roha taluka.
9. *Koralwadi,* 3 kms from Tara, off the Panvel-Goa highway, Panvel taluka.
10. *Bhanubhaiwadi,* 3 kms off the Panvel-Goa highway, east from Tara, Panvel taluka.
11. *Hemdi,* 15 kms from Pen on the Khopoli road, Pen taluka.

Village-level Data

Table Columns:-

1 = Village (Vil)

2 = No. of households (Hse)

3 = No. of land-owning families (L)

4 = No. of houses with electricity (E)

5 = Water Supply (WS)

W = well, BW = borewell, T = tapwater, C = canal.

6 = Political Party supported (PP)
Cong-I = Congress I, SKP = Shetkari-Kamgari Paksh, KMS = Kashtakari Mukti Sanghatana.

7 = Clan Names (CN)
J = Jadhar, Ka = Kapre, Ko = Koli, Ku = Kulwe, P = Pawar, Wg = Wagmare, Wh = Waghule, Wk = Walekde

8 = Communities in contact (CC)
Ma = Maharthas, Mu = Muslims, Bu = Buddhists, Ag = Agris, Tk = Thakkurs, Mr = Marwaris, Dh = Dhangars, Ga = Gawlis.

Table: Village-level Data

	1 (Vil)	2 (HSE)	3 (L)	4 (E)	5 (WS)	6 (PP)	7 (CN)	8 (CC)
1.	Pui	46	2	6	W,C	Cong-I	Wg,P,J	Ma,Mu,Bu
2.	Shedashi	59	36	Nil	W	Cong-I	Wg,P	Ma,Th,Ag, Mr
3.	Bhuneshwar	22	Nil	Nil	T	Cong-I now SKP	Wk,P	Ma
4.	Khairatwadi	15	2	15	T	Cong-I and SKP	Wg,P	Ma,Ag
5.	Berle	108	13	23	BW	Cong-I	Wg,J	Ag
6.	Killa	30	1	3	T	SKP and Cong-I	Wg,P,J,Ko	Ma
7.	Barsoli	52	Nil	15	T	SKP and Cong-I	Wg,P,J,Ku	Ma
8.	Palekhurd	45	3	7	W	SKP now Cong-I	Wg,P,J, Ku, Ka	Ma,Th,Dh
9.	Koralwadi	28	2	Nil	W, BW	Cong-I, SKP, KMS	Wg,P,J	Ma,Ga,Th
10.	Bhanubhai-wadi	30	Nil	2	T	SKP, Cong-I KMS	Wg,P,	Ag, Mu
11.	Hemdi	55	14	Nil	T	Cong-I	Wg,P,J,Wh	Ma

Some Socio-religious Customs

(a) Religious practises. (b) Belief in the Bhagat. (c) Festivals.

Pui

(a) Visit the shrine of Vithal and Rakhumai at Pandharpur at least once a year.
(b) Go to both, the bhagat and the city doctor.
(c) Ganpati, Shimga, Gatari Amavasya, Pitra Amavasya and Kav Kavicha.

Shedashi

(a) Make annual trips to Pandharpur.
(b) Go to the bhagat as well as the city doctor.
(c) Ganpati, Shimga, Gatari Amavasya, Diwali and Pitra Amavasya.

Bhuneshwar

(a) Go to the shrine of Goad Shiva at Mahadev Mandir village once a month.
(b) believe in both, bhagat and doctor.
(c) Pitra Amavasya, Ganpati, Shimga, Gatari Amavasya and Diwali.

Khairatwadi

(a) Go to the shrine of Ekwira Ai at Karla Phata on the Lonavala Road and the Mari Ai shrine at Khopoli Road at least once a year.
(b) Believe in both, bhagat and doctor.
(c) Ganpati, Gatari Amavasya, Shivratri and Pitra Amavasya.

Berle

(a) Are devotees of Ramdas Swami, a religious organization

based in Raigad, have given up drinking, have monthly get togethers at Kone village for Bhajans. Also visit Pandharpur.

(b) Do not believe in the bhagat.

(c) Ganpati, Shimga, Gatari Amavsya, Diwali, Pitra Amavasya.

Killa

(a) Go for the Mahadev mandir Yatra of Lord Shankar every Mahashivratri and also believe in Vithoba of Pandharpur.

Many also believe in Saibaba and visit Shirdi. Some women claim to do the Santoshi Mata Vrata and Tuesday fasts but not the Karva Chauth.

(b) Have a strong belief in the bhagat but also visit the doctor when required.

(c) Gatari Amavasya, Shivratri, Shimga and Diwali.

Barsoli

(a) Go to Vithoba's shrine at Sadgaon (near Khopoli). Their own village has a shrine of Mari Ai and the government has built them a temple.

(b) Believe in the bhagat as well as the city doctor.

(c) Ganpati, Shivratri, Gatari and Pitra Amavsya, Shimga and Diwali.

Palekhurd

(a. Go to Mahadev Wadi and Khamb (near Pui) for an annual yatra once a year.

(b) Believe in the bhagat as well as the city doctor.

(c) Shimga, Gatari Amavsya and Mahashivratri.

Koralwadi

(a) Go to the Barapada Uroos festival in January, Apta during

Chaitya and also the Tara utsav.

(b) Believe in both, bhagat and doctor.

(c) Ganpati, Shimga, Mahashivratri, Gatari Amavasya, Pitra Amavasya and Diwali.

Bhanubhaiwadi

(a) Go for their Yatra to Ladavli on the Rasayani road, some go to Shankarachi dev and we have a temple of Sai-Bhavani Goddess and go to Maruti and Ganpati temples on Tuesdays. Uroos festival in the Barapada Muslim village is also patronised.

(b) Believe in both, the bhagat and the doctor.

(c) Shimga, Diwali, Shivratri, Pitra and Gatari Amavasya.

Hemdi

(a) Have regular bhajan sessions, make annual trips to Pandharpur, resistant to the overtures made by some Protestant groups at conversions.

(b) Believe in both, the bhagat and the city doctor.

(c) Ganpati, Diwali, Shimga, Gatari Amavasya, and Kav Kausha.

Demands from Governmental and Non-governmental Organizations

Pui

(a) An uphill road from the canal towards their settlement.

(b) Separate dali zamin in the name of each individual.

(c) A government school up to the SSC level.

(d) Gaothan land which is divided between two gram panchayats to be put on their name.

(e) A cremation area of their own.

(f) Money to improve houses and build shops.

Shedashi

(a) Land for all.

(b) Vegetable gardens.

(c) Goats and bullocks.

(d) Work in towns and cities.

(e) Help in getting out of loan traps, for those who have mortgaged their land.

Bhuneshwar

(a) Separate dali zamin in the name of each individual.

(b) A government school.

(c) A water connections.

Khairatwadi

(a) Government must provide them with land.

(b) Non-governmental agencies can help in providing technical skills in using the land productively.

(c) Breaking loan traps and retrieving lost land.

(d) Non-governmental agencies to help in the field of education.

Berle

(a) Jobs in the public and private sector.

(b.) Help from non-governmental agencies in applying and getting these jobs.

(c) Land back on their own name as the Thalati had tricked and usurped their property.

(d) Improving their houses (which have been built with bad material due to corrupt officials).

Killa

(a) Help in the field of education from governmental and non-governmental organizations.

(b) Land, which is now controlled by the Marathas, must be put back in their name.

(c) Non-interference by the Marathas of Killa village in their voting practices. The Kathkaris want to vote the Shetkari Kamgar Paksha but the Marathas force them to vote for the Congress-I.

(d) Pucca houses for all. The control for this should not be given to the Marathas who control the panchayat.

Barsoli

(a) Work in factories.

(b) Work for children in factories not as labourers but salary earners.

(c) Bullocks and implements for cultivation.

(d) Goat schemes for additional money.

(e) Good education for children.

Palekhurd

(a) A job which gives continuous income, not daily wages.

(b) Help in getting out of the habit of drinking.

(c) Government must provide streetlights and water as after holi in summer water is a problem.

(d) Education and regular jobs for the children.

Koralwadi

a. Land on individual ownership basis.

b. Regular income generating jobs.

c. Revival of schemes like poultry co-operatives.

d. Education for children.

Bhanubhaiwadi

(a) Poultry co-operative scheme.

(b) Education for children.

(c) Dali land for all members.

(d) Bullocks for cultivation.

Hemdi

(a) Water-pumps for rice fields.

(b) Money to start business of goats for selling milk.

(c) Electric connections in each home.

(d) Education for children.

(e) Land for all members in the settlement.

APPENDIX III.

CENSUS DATA

Table I: Raigad District Population[11]

	Total	Decadal/ Difference	Percentage Change
1951	9,09,083	1,03,926	12.91
1961	10,58,855	1,49,772	16.48
1971	12,63,003	2,04,148	19.28
1981	14,86,452	2,23,449	17.69
1991	18,14,628	3,28,176	22.08

Table II: Population Density[12]

	Sq.kms	Pop./Sq.kms	Resident Villages	Resident Towns
Total				
Raigad Dt.				
Total	7,148.0	208	1,827	16
Rural	7,014.7	182	1,827	
Urban	133.3	1574		
Panvel Taluk				
Total	578.3	349	173	2
Rural	560.1	287	173	
Urban	18.2	2,236	173	
Pen Taluk				
Total	498.5	239	149	1
Rural	488.7	213	149	
Urban	9.8	1,504		
Roha Taluk				
Total	632.4	171	160	1
Rural	611.7	158	160	
Urban	20.7	569		

Source : Raigad Zilla Gazetteer, Maharashtra Sharn, 1993 (Marathi)

Table III: Percent Change in Population[13]

	1951-61	1961-71	1971-81	1981-91
Maharashtra State	23.60	27.45	24.54	25.43
Raigad District	16.48	19.28	17.69	22.08
Panvel Taluka	26.25	28.58	34.88	38.91
Pen Taluka	19.43	20.39	18.74	23.66
Roha Taluka	17.28	13.71	19.61	27.17

REFERENCES

1. Claude Levi-Strauss, "Anthropology: Its Achievements and Future", *Current Anthropology,* 1966, Vol.7, p. 124-7.
2. Marvin Harris, *Cultural Materialism: The Struggle for a Science of Culture,* Random House, New York, 1980, p. 32.
3. J. Pathy, *Ethnic Minorities, op. cit.,* p. 43.
4. Jawaharlal Handoo, *op. cit.,* p. 38.
5. Robert Redfield, *The Little Community Viewpoints for the Study of the Human Whole,* University of Chicago Press, Chicago, 1962.
6. M. M. Postan, *The Historical Method in Social Science,* The University Press, Cambridge, England, 1939, p. 36.
7. Robert Redfield, *op. cit.* p.104.
8. For a more detailed discussion cf. Rudolf C. Heredia, *Voluntary Action and Development: Towards a Praxis for Non-Government Agencies,* Concept, New Delhi, 1988, pp. 25-31.
9. M.N.Srinivas *et.al.* eds, *The Field Worker and the Field: Problems and Challenges in Sociological Investigation,* Oxford University Press, Delhi, 1979, p.9.
10. Ref. YMC pamphlet, National house, 6, Tulloch Road, Bombay 400 039.
11. *Raigad Zilla Gazetteer,* Maharastra Shasan, 1993 (Marathi), p.193.
12. *ibid* p. 256-8.
13. *ibid* p. 194.

3

RECONSTRUCTING THE KATHKARI PROFILE

INTRODUCTION

Raigad district is part of the Konkan region of coastal Maharashtra. Beginning across from Bombay, this district runs just south of New Bombay for about 150 kms along the coast, and on an average about 50 kms inland. In 1991 it had a population of 18,24,628 in an area of 7,148 sq.kms. The flat and narrow coastal plain is indented with creeks and inlets while the Western Ghats rise sharply and steeply from this plain to mark the eastern boundary of this district.

Until the 1970s it was called Colaba district, but then was renamed in 1981 after the medieval capital of the Maharata hero Shivaji which was within its boundaries. Now the abandoned mountain fortress survives as an historical reminder of a once glorious but long lost past. Until very recently this was considered a backward area of Maharashtra, and along with the rest of the Konkan coast was one of the main suppliers of labour to the industrial centres in and around Bombay. But now there is an accelerated spill over from these centres old and new into Raigad district causing a marked increase of immigration into the district, and a steep increase in its population.

The Kathkaris also called Kathodis, are a small scheduled tribe in western India, scattered across the districts of south Gujarat and northern Maharashtra, with a sprinkling in Rajasthan. They are most concentrated in the district of Thana and more so in Raigad. Kathkaris are officially categorized among the most backward of the scheduled tribes. That, in Raigad now, they find themselves in one of the fastest developing areas in the country and perhaps in all of South Asia is part of the cruel irony of their fate. For New Bombay, the counter-magnet to the older metropolis, being developed in this district with the latest modern , hightech, capital intensive investment, this means speeding the entire area into the twenty-first century, leaving no space for these tribals who were once proud hunter-gatherers and are today reduced to being migrant labour.

At present the total Kathkari population is about 1,25,000 and their percentage in Raigad is about ten. Some of the demographic details concerning them have been culled from the Census data and presented in the appendix of the previous chapter. But our concern here is less with their demographic profile, than their vulnerable status, culturally, economically and politically. For after they have been marginalized, they are now being forcibly assimilated at the very bottom of the social ladder. This is precisely the kind of situation that poses most sharply the questions regarding ethnic identity and human dignity that are the focus of this study.

In this chapter we shall attempt to reconstruct the Kathkari profile from the meager documentation available, so as to set them in their contemporary context.

CRITIQUING THE SOURCES

The self-perception of the Kathkaris, like any other human group, has been influenced by the attitudes of neighbouring communities which interact with them, and these have had a major impact on their identity and notions of self-worth. But besides these communities, one also finds the presence of specialized agencies which work with and for the Kathkaris, having varied intentions in this endeavor, political, religious or altruistic. These agencies too, in their own way, have contributed to the development of the self-perception of the Kathkaris, often reinforcing negative stereotypes.

This happens because they enter into the traditional discourse on the Kathkaris which originates in popular non-Kathkari attitudes along with those that emerge with the experience of the agencies themselves. In the case of the latter, historical and anthropological statements play an important role, as they are referred to and accepted as being more authoritative, backed as they are with professional expertise or the confidence of a supposedly superior understanding.

They become major sources of information on the community and leave their mark, directly or indirectly on the perceptions and attitudes of all those who interact with them. The problem begins when the readers ignore or are not aware of the various subjective factors embedded in these texts. It may be difficult for them to believe that the information given can be tied up with personal opinions and often the two are not distinguished.

One may also ignore the observation that the so called "objective facts" presented are shaped by the interests of the authors or unconsciously guided by particular circumstances. This holds true whether one is referring to a circular handed out by Christian missionaries or a Ph.D thesis written by a scholar. At the same time, it must be acknowledged, that such documents are valuable sources of information, despite of the various factors operating and they do give interesting and valuable insights into this community.

The Missionary Venture

The earliest report on the Kathkaris seems to be by a certain Major A. Mackintosh referred to by John Wilson, whose "Account of the Waralis and Katodis—two of the Forest Tribes of the northern Konkan", was read to the Bombay Branch of the Royal Asiatic Society in 1841.[1] Wilsons's own account is based on Mackintosh and his own notes made after a few encounters with these tribesmen on his travels through this region. It takes the form of a personal narrative of a missionary interested in "their religious sentiments and practices".[2]

The interrogations he faithfully records are indeed quaint, and he trusts "will not be altogether uninteresting to the Christian mind"![3] But final judgement he makes is severe:

> They are the most degraded body of natives with whom I am acquainted.... they live, as outcasts, near villages inhabited by other classes of the community. They are held in great abhorrence by the common agriculturalists, and particularly by the Brahmans; and their residences are wretched beyond belief. Their miserable units are situated where all the refuse of the village is thrown, and they have companionship with all that is impure. Looking to the position in which they are found, and to the profession of families an intercourse with malignant spirits which they make, we can scarcely fail to associate them with the words of the Revelation--"without are dogs and sorcerers".[4]

Obviously the ethnocentric lack of empathy betrayed here makes it quite impossible for this pious missionary to bridge the communication gap between his world and the tribal Kathkaris, whom he briefly encounters. His real sources of information are outsiders to the tribe, and though some of the ethnographic detail he reports are verified by later records, his final condemnation of the Kathkaris as "very depraved, as well as debased",[5] only echoes an uncritical and unfair stereotype.

However, in fairness to Wilson we must also remark that even he had

> no doubt, that if ground were assigned to them on easy terms by the government, and if they were put in possession of the means of bringing it under cultivation, and prevented from dissipating these means by a resort to the liquor-shop, they would be content to establish themselves as a body of agriculturalists.[6]

And he is happy with the "paternal concern" the authorities are showing to this end.

If we have quoted Wilson at length it is because he provides us with an excellent illustration of what not to do in our attempt to reconstruct the Kathkari profile later. For we must not only contextualize the sources of our information, we must be equally sensitive to how our own context may prejudice our perceptions.

To contextualize the documentation reviewed here a short historical outline of the Kune mission would be well in order. For it is the missionary encounter that provides a vital source of information and insight for the tribals in this country. It serves as a crucial complement to government records that originated in the colonial enterprise. Hence the prominence given to them in this review.

Situated on the crest of the Western Ghats, just off the Bombay-Pune road, the Kune mission was begun in the foothills by a Jesuit of St. Xavier's College, Bombay, Brother Leonard Zimmer in 1894. The move to Kune village in 1904 was an attempt to settle and stabilize the tribals who had converted to Catholicism. A school was started in the same year along with a coir-matting factory. Subsequently other economic activities included making of cotton and woollen carpets. But despite many years of service the mission never quite took root among the Kathkaris and it was eventually closed down officially in 1982.

Here we are not attempting to make an assessment of the missionaries, but rather to critique some of the crucial documentation they have left us, so as to understand this community better.

The Zimmermann Report

The first document for discussion in this essay is "The Khandala Kathkaris", an address by Rev. Father R. Zimmermann S.J. read on 28th February 1921.[7]

It is difficult to say whether the references used by the author influenced his opinions or that his personal observations made him read them in a particular way, but the written document is testimony to the argument made above, that personal interests or specific circumstances influence such works and misrepresent the subjects of their study.

Throughout the document there are constant references made to the Kathkari's "inherent laziness", "weakness",[8] "high suggestibility",[9] and "undisciplined temper".[10] The Kathkari is presented as an impulsive though "mild, gentle and inoffensive" person,[11] whose free and undisciplined spirit has to be carefully tackled if one wants to bring it under control.[12] The Kathkari thus comes across as a contradictory being who is both submissive and resistant to authority, has a mentality which is "extraordinarily unsophisticated"[13] even though possessing the "qualities of a democrat".[14] At every description one senses an attempt to portray the Kathkari as someone who needs external intervention to become 'civilized'. Anecdotes are provided which further emphasize this perception:

> Their knowledge is so primitive that their brains must be very little burdened. Naturally do they of their own account not see the need for more knowledge either. The Missionary in charge of the Kuna settlement near Khandala relates: ... 'the Kathkaris did not like their children to be in school... I told them they did not know what was good for them, and then collected them in the schoolroom, old and young. Then I set the master writing the Marathi alphabet on the blackboard, and teaching them what the letters meant. The whole crowd roared with laughter.[15]

Narrating such an incident without taking into consideration the cultural problems faced by the community in a rapidly changing scenario and the difficulties in adjustment they experienced, can only reinforce the exaggerated image of a people who have the mentality "of an extraordinarily unsophisticated and unprejudiced description".[16]

From here one is led into a discussion on how to control or deal with them. It is clearly stated that because of the "undisciplined character of the people", a "mere mechanical outside check" is useless.[17] One is advised to intimately enter into their life and it is only then that "one can secure any hold on them at all".[18] The impression that the Kune settlement had managed quite well in this regard is conveyed through a debate on the classification of the Kathkaris as a professionally criminal tribe by M. Kennedy.[19] Though Zimmermann rejects this classification he acknowledges that they may be "addicted to stealing on a small scale",[20] but also adds that they cannot be called "wild or lawless".[21] Then again he accepts that the Kathkaris occasionally do commit some crimes. This is followed by the assertion:

> since the Kuna settlement had been established on a sound footing, Kathkari crime had ceased in the Khandalla village area. The government was on one occasion able to reward Kathkaris for help in thief catching; at another time they were invited to join the police force. All this does not however absolve them from a tribal tendency to grabbing, filching or pilfering, which is successfully checked and eventually given up only in the settlement.[22]

The document emphasizes the importance of the Kune settlement in improving the life of the Kathkaris. It is taken for granted that traditional Kathkari life is a primitive and undeveloped one. This can be clearly seen in the author's observation that "... the jumping habit (sic) is so strong with them that only with the greatest difficulty and forbearance they can be brought to a settled life".[23]

The author definitely writes with a confidence which comes from the belief that his lifestyle is the one they must emulate. Yet, the experience of the missionaries reveals how difficult it was for them to actually bring the community into their fold. One learns that the Kathkaris often left the settlement *en masse* a number of times and even when they agreed to stay on, they needed an occasional day off in the forest.

While the author acknowledges that the Kathkaris are really "children of the forest" there is no attempt to accept this as a valid way of life. This can be verified by the lack of any mention of the forests being taken over by governmental authorities and the consequent alienation of the people from the traditional means of their livelihood. These are events which would not have been omitted had a more sympathetic outlook been taken by the author to the Kathkari way of life. The author describes the Kathkari's attitude to work in the saying:

> "Do as little as ever you can, and get that done by another man".

He goes on to assert that for " centuries they were unaccustomed to application to work",[24] and once again exposes his prejudice. Obviously, his understanding of work is a limited one, acceptable to the ethics of his society alone. The detailed description which he himself provides of hunting, food-gathering, fishing, etc., performed by Kathkari men and women do not come under his category.

The conflict between the two lifestyles represented by the mission and the community can be consistently observed, e.g., in the Kathkari children's resistance to corporal punishment, as the "slightest slap would make them yell as if they were being murdered",[25] or in the incident when a group of drunken Kathkaris destroyed the yarn for weaving, which was "the very means of their livelihood".[26] This incident is used to portray the "undisciplined temper"[27] of the Kathkaris, for which they are made to feel sorry afterwards, but the possibility of viewing it as a form of protest or an expression of frustration due to the adjustments demanded from them is not considered at all. The Kathkari is only seen as a "creature of impulse"[28] with little traces of rationality. All this is accompanied by glorifying the role of the mission in uplifting these fallen people.

The concluding paragraph underlines the attitude of the mission towards the Kathkaris as a paternalistic one, viewing the community as if they were children who require careful upbringing.

> Long and detailed experience has shown that he (the Kathkari) is capable of responding to the light when it once shines upon him.... for the heroically unselfish worker who has to offer a higher life, and can abide the time of harvest, the Kathkaris prove an object of attention and love not less worthy than any other member of the human race.[29]

But as the history of the Kune mission shows, Fr. Zimmermann's optimism proved to be mistaken. Perhaps the "free jungle spirit", that he talks about, was too strong, and all the tensions between the two ways of life, hinted at in the document, began to manifest themselves on a much larger scale, leading to the eventual closing down of the mission many years later.

The Jesuits withdrew from Kune officially, in 1982. It was felt that the type of activities being carried out for the benefit of the people concerned showed no appreciable positive results.[30] Perhaps the mission set goals for the Kathkaris which were too difficult for them to achieve given their historical limitations. But in any case the fact that they were not really understood by even those who worked so dedicatedly for them is sadly apparent.

The Mission Survey

A major source of information on the Kune mission and its relationship with the Kathkaris is a report written by Fr. Anthony Ribas in 1976, six years before the shutting down of the mission. The " Socio-economic Survey of the Kune Mission—Part 1",[31] gives a brief history of the Kune mission and a description of the Kathkaris.

The image of the community in this report is a virtual reproduction of that in Fr. Zimmermann's document, but when it comes to a discussion on their interaction with the mission one finds a more complex picture emerging. This is because the report is much more recent, and has many years of experience behind it. It must be noted though, that the complexity of its vision is not because it looks at the Kathkaris in a new light, but due to the contradictions it perceived in the mission's interaction itself.

On one hand we have the Kathkaris portrayed as helpless and weak, justifying the help provided by the mission[32] and on the other, we find the report condemning the overdependence of the Kathkaris, and accusing the mission of spoiling them.[33] In fact in the early seventies, one finds a major change in policy under the leadership of Fr. Anthony Ribas, S.J., when the emphasis was put on making them "self-reliant and responsible".[34]

What is particularly interesting is the section which compares the Kathkaris of the Kune mission and those of the plains. In a way the report admits to the limitations of the mission when it points out that in spite of its influence the Kathkaris of the mission retain their former "defects",[35] while those from the plains are more industrious and "self-respecting".[36] They are said to have their own livestock and lands, are proud of their independence and are able to preserve their dignity *vis-a-vis* the Marathas.

This is certainly an honest exercise in self-criticism. But then, we also find the report accusing the Kathkaris of a lack of unity and the prevalence of jealousy among them, which are seen as major obstacles in their "progress".[37] A more detailed analysis of these two groups of Kathkaris would have helped the mission change its policies much earlier and become a more influential factor in their lives.

There is also a rather unclear analysis of the problems faced by those converted to Christianity, where their practice of beef-eating is seen as an important cause for other Kathkaris not interacting with them. It is stated that "this attitude is fast disappearing because all frequent the same public hotels and eat food from the same vessels".[38] This seems to be a rather simplistic observation, whereas it could have been used to get some important insights into the reservations faced by the

Kathkaris in having a more involved relationship with the mission.

The fact that among the Kathkaris there is an indigenous division which practices beef-eating is also ignored, though this was common knowledge even then. This indigenous group was considered of lower status within Kathkari social relations. This could have contributed to the half-hearted participation of the other Kathkaris in mission's activities, even though the help provided to them may have been well appreciated. However, they were rather hastily dubbed "rice Christians"[39] and the "shallow faith of the Kathkaris" was evident in incidents where they were accused of taking part in a Muslim ceremony "just for the food and clothing".[40]

Through the report one learns that the creation of the mission at Kune in 1894 was largely the result of Br. Leonard Zimmer, who made a sincere attempt to get involved with the Kathkaris by learning Marathi, spending time with them in their villages and participating in their festivals. In fact, when in 1913, the Jesuit fathers were "fed up" with the Kathkaris and were ready to shut down the mission, "probably because of their reluctance to accept Christianity",[41] it was Br. Zimmer who pointed out that the failure was more due to the "frequent change of personnel and the inability to understand the people" combined "with a lack of tact in dealing with them".[42] On his persistence, the mission was allowed to continue.

Br. Zimmer had also managed to get land for the tribals as the government had restricted their free movement in the forests and was forcing them to settle down. Concrete attempts were also made to help them adjust to the changing economic situation through starting production centers of clothes, carpets etc.. Their conversion continued simultaneously and, the report informs us that in 1916, 150 Kathkaris were baptized, a minuscule part of their population.

As mentioned earlier, the report is critical of the overdependence fostered by the mission, but at the same time one also finds a tendency to present the Kathkaris as completely helpless without its involvement. For example, it mentions that after the death of Fr. More in 1965, "their entire life was reportedly thrown out of gear",[43] they lost all that they had saved over the years and lived "listlessly, until the advent of the new director of the mission".

This report also ends with misplaced optimism as it discusses the state of affairs in 1972 claiming that "on the whole the mission has acquired a firm foundation and the future looks bright",[44] quite contrary to what really happened.

Both the documents discussed above may have contributed to a negative perception of the Kathkaris on the part of those who interacted with them. This may not have been intentional and certainly does not mean that the interaction was negative. On the contrary, the help provided by the mission and later on, by other voluntary organizations could have been very important interventions to help the community adjust to changing times.

But this interaction did not necessarily imply an attitude which was always beneficial to the Kathkaris. That is to say, the required understanding and respect which any distinctive way of life deserves may have been lacking, even as the help provided was important. The ideal of self-reliance and independence could not be actually fulfilled because both these qualities are closely linked to questions of identity and dignity. If enough attention is not paid to the latter any help provided is bound to backfire. This was clearly seen in the contradictory experiences reflected in the report and the confusion which prevailed in the mission's relationship with the Kathkaris.

The documents just discussed were discourses closely intertwined with actual interaction with the Kathkaris. The opinions shared were based on experiences which grew out of a close relationship with the tribals. Even if the authors may not have been directly involved, they based their writings on personal observations, other written material and most importantly, the viewpoints of fieldworkers and those associated with the mission.

An Anthropological Approach

Scientific Subjectivity

The next document for analysis is different from the above in as much as it claims to be an objective and scientific work, it is a Ph.D. thesis on the Kathkaris written in 1934 by an anthropologist A.N. Weling.[45] This book is extremely important as a source of information for both students and social workers. Nearly all voluntary organizations working with the tribe use it as a major reference. With its stamp of scientific expertise it becomes a very authoritative piece of work.

Social Anthropology has been traditionally seen as a science which documents and studies tribal life. Its word is seen as reliable because it claims to be objective and detached, features ideally demanded from scientific works. It is only very recently that this authority has been challenged and the weaknesses of the discipline exposed. The biases hidden within supposedly neutral statements and the western perspective which overwhelms such writing have been seen as the major factors responsible for portraying non-western societies in an ahistorical manner and for being consciously or unconsciously blind to the processes of economic and political domination which have always been present in the experience of these societies.

Indigenous cultures in India cannot be studied with the same theoretical tools developed for analysing similar societies in other parts of the world, especially with the caste dynamics at work here. Yet we find monographs written in exactly the same manner as say, in Africa or South America. Weling's work too reflects such an approach and the following analysis makes an attempt to caution the reader against such influences.

Yet one must acknowledge at the start that the author has often shown some excellent insights into the community, especially in his thesis about the heterogeneity of Kathkari identity and in his observations on the capacity of the Kathkari to adapt to changing situations. Both these points have been incorporated into the later section on the history of the community.

Thus the critique here does not aim at revealing limitations in this particular work by Weling per se, but rather shedding some light on the problems associated with all such monographs, which have to be seen in a wider context of the methodological debates in anthropology.

Oversimplified Stereotypes

Weling may not use a language which blatantly labels the Kathkaris in negative stereotypes, but he often fails to present them with all their complexities. As many anthropological documents do to their objects of study, he also tends to portray the Kathkaris as completely moulded by the natural environment, paying very little attention to political processes which were changing all aspects of their life during the time he was writing his thesis.

This was of course, in tune with traditional anthropological research which idealized the close relationship with nature that such people had, without acknowledging the conflict of interest around natural resources which has always been intrinsic to their history. This tendency is part of a larger venture to view such communities not as historical beings who have also responded to change, often by resisting domination in their own way, but as static cultures having fixed identities which have to be integrated into the dominant processes of social change. These processes are of course, uncritically accepted as universally prevalent and uniformly valid.

Thus we find Weling asserting that:

> Every aspect of the Kathkari life is to some extent influenced by the geographic environment of the country... How far he has yielded to or is molded by pure geographic and climatic environment must be judged in the light of his inherited and acquired physical and mental characteristics.... [46]

Such a statement is a platitude. After all nature has played an important role in shaping all cultures. But stating it in this manner has an underlying ideological intention. While western societies will be seen as active players in their historical development as cultures which have moulded the forces of nature, non-western ones, especially tribal ones, have been denied this privilege and have been viewed purely as geographically determined entities.

This perception has far-reaching consequences, especially when used in writing their history. They will never be portrayed as active agents but as passive or subservient creatures of their cultures, and when this self-understanding is internalized by them, their very identity becomes threatened as they are subsumed within dominant cultures and only in subordinate roles.

A certain ethnocentrism can be seen in very innocuous sounding statements. "The black or dark-brown skin of the Kathkari has kept to its present hue as the scorching climate of the hills and the hot rays of the tropical sun falling on his bare skin are detrimental to the improvement of pigmentation."[47] Or "his low culture is principally responsible for the poor type of dwelling and poverty in dress and furniture."[48]

Ethnographic Detail

The monograph is written very much in the fashion of most anthropological writings of the time and there are separate sections on "physical features", "technical culture", "social organization", "marriage and birth", "death and funeral" and "arts and sciences". A preoccupation with recording details of cultural life leaves very little space for analysis. In fact it is only in the very short conclusion that we get a picture of the Kathkaris in a more dynamic light.

Weling states:

> Wherever I found a Kathkari, I found him in a comparatively prosperous condition. It is certain that all through the year he

> manages to support himself and his family....[49]

He feels that the aspiration of the Kathkari, then, was for —

> developing from hunting to the settled agricultural stage. His immediate superior is the Kunbi--the Hindu agriculturist--who so out-weighs him numerically that in the clash of cultures of the two parties the Kathkari shall have to either adopt completely the Kunbi culture and be merged in the class, or, stick to the original hunting stage and possibly be eliminated.[50]

This is certainly an insightful observation, and the use of the phrase "clash of cultures" is particularly significant. It is a marked departure from his predominantly diffusionist vision making him talk of imitation and "taking on" of upper caste traits.[51] While such a process is a historical fact, it has many other dimensions to it, which are not adequately brought out when seen only from a diffusionist stand or in terms of caste mobility.

The moral superiority behind upper-caste attitudes during interaction with the Kathkaris, even if the Kathkaris are not considered ritually impure, and the consequent decrease in their perceptions of self-worth, are points not covered. The fact that the "taking on of upper caste traits" is a result of economic compulsion is not taken into consideration and a certain voluntarism is imputed to the community's motivation.

This only exaggerates the image of Hinduism as having an "integrative" and "assimilative" force, and ignores the economic and cultural processes which make such a movement happen. The overimportance given to the collection of cultural traits as if they are totally divorced from economic and political processes, made Weling blind to interventions made by governmental agencies which drastically altered the lifestyle of the Kathkari.

Exogenous Factors

Studies of the region show that the cutting of trees for ship-building and the network of the Great Indian Peninsular railway, played an important role in the landscape of the region, and precipitated the commercial penetration into forests, which was one of the factors in initiating the absorption of forest-dependent communities as labourers in larger markets. Forests were fenced off from them and viewed as a resource for the market economy, cutting off the tribals from a traditional source of their livelihood.

The people were forced to settle down but as land became more scarce, they had to fight against being deprived from this means of livelihood too. The government integrated them into the market economy so that they could be taxed and the banning of local liquor in favour of licensed production centres, was an important move in this direction, as it ensured their insertion into the monetary system of exchange.[52]

The limitations imposed on the movement of the Kathkaris in the forests deprived them of the chance of maintaining an autonomy from other communities even as they interacted with them. When Weling feels that the Kathkaris, to survive, have to assimilate themselves into the dominant Kunbi lifestyle, he does not mention all the circumstances which might have forced such a change. The alienation from forests, forceful settlement of the people and the development of land as a scarce commodity are events which do not find mention in Weling's thesis.

But in all fairness to his work it must be mentioned again that this is one among the very few sources of information on this community and certainly the most exhaustive one. Once its limitations are viewed in a wider context, it becomes an invaluable resource for any inquiry into the Kathkaris.

Concluding the Review

The purpose of reviewing the three documents was to show the links of official and scientific discourse on the Kathkaris with the popular one as embedded in intercommunity relations of all kinds. This was done mainly because the prevalent general attitudes towards the Kathkaris is a rather negative one. So much so that the community itself lives without much dignity because of the poor notions of self-worth internalized by them.

The overall framework of this inquiry is based on questions of identity and dignity of the tribe because it is felt that their economic deprivation and cultural alienation is organically related to a weak cultural and political identity. The need to see economic deprivation and cultural alienation as working together in keeping the tribe where they are is a point which cannot be underestimated.

The documents have, in their own way, contributed to such an alienation, making a critical reading of them an important task. The point was not to show the weaknesses of these particular writings in themselves, but of cautioning the reader against the subjectivities embedded in all such works. Only then can a reading be made which sees the Kathkaris in a different light, a task which is attempted in the following sections.

A HISTORICAL RECONSTRUCTION

The discussion here cannot be referred to as an accurate historical account of the Kathkaris. It is certainly not a rigorous inquiry into their way of past with the intention of presenting a detailed description of their way of life through the ages, nor can it boast of an exhaustive research on the history of the region to shed light on the story of the Kathkaris. That would require an effort more specialized and demanding, especially as it would then be expected to make definitive statements.

Questioning the Assumptions

In keeping with the assumptions of the entire project, outlined earlier, our attempt is to provide for a historical perspective on the Kathkaris by attempting to counteract the image of a stagnant cultural entity which has become so widespread. It attempts to question the belief that the Kathkaris are in a subordinate position today due to their inherent characteristics which are attributed to a fixed cultural identity linked to an unchanging past, a constructed past which justifies the labelling of these people as primitive and backward.

This has been done by making an alternative reading of those documents which have been specifically written on the Kathkaris, and have themselves been responsible for presenting an ahistorical picture of the people, as has been discussed earlier. Our analysis should hopefully make an attempt to get out of the limitations which exist in such discourses with the objective of stimulating further discussion and presenting a perspective for substantiation by subsequent studies, or for critiquing their inadequacies.

An Alternative Perspective

This attempt then is only a small step towards writing a history of this community. We are aware of the difficulties in claiming any account as being the authentic one. But as our immediate concerns are linked to the proposition that the present image of the Kathkaris is a distorted one, any attempt to rectify it is a welcome move. And even if it will be difficult to make any definitive statements, since our focus is on evolving new perspectives on the Kathkaris, we still feel that this does not deny any legitimacy to the endeavour here.

Not an Isolated Community

This presentation keeps in mind the following points: firstly, the Kathkaris have not been an isolated community as there is indication of their economic and cultural exchange with neighbouring ethnic groups in the region, for a considerable period of time. Yet they have also maintained a distinct ethnic identity. The necessity of certain commodities like salt, oil and cloth, ensured such interdependence, while the forests provided alternatives which made them relatively independent.

The term Kathkari itself implies an exchange of a commodity called "catechu". Resin from the Khair tree which was at one time abundant in the forests around is used in betelnut chewing. The extraction of this product gave the people a name, and indicates one specialized activity through which interaction with other groups could take place. Though the forest product "catechu" could not have been a basis of every day economic exchange with neighbouring groups as say, toddy would have. It is more likely that there were special intermediate groups which entered into the relation and who were part of a wider market.

> "Catechu" may have been one among other forest produce, like firewood or wild fruit, used for exchange and could have co-existed with other occupations for survival which did not imply an exchange relation, like fishing or food-gathering, making way for both, an Interdependent as well as independent existence.

Exchange Relations

Secondly, while exchange relations thus accounted for their contact with other social groups, the forests provided for a large number of needs and limited their interaction. Of course, there is a danger of oversimplification here, as distinctions between social groups do not have a basis only in material factors. After all, the Thakkurs, traditional toddy tappers of the region, and the Kathkaris did share the same environment, and yet sustained separate identities. But in spite of this one can confidently say that the forests still had more significance for the latter.

This can be understood if we consider the fact that the Kathkaris had maintained a strict taboo on toddy making while their own needs of drinking were satisfied by the Thakkurs. Toddy-making among the Thakkurs had important consequences on their history, as toddy being the basis of everyday interaction with other communities, increased their contact with settled agrarian groups and thereby their status *vis-a-vis* the Kathkaris. Subsequently during the period of colonialism, the same activity made them relatively more prosperous, while the Kathkaris became increasingly dependent on labour. After all "catechu" making was never really a basis of everyday exchange and did not fulfil all their needs, and once the forests came to be controlled by outsiders their independence was no longer possible.

Thus historically, in spite of the other complexities involved, it cannot be denied that the forests, by providing alternative sources of livelihood did limit the possibilities of traditional and obligatory exchange relations and facilitated a more independent existence for the Kathkaris.

Autonomy and Interdependence

Thirdly, this relation of autonomy and interdependence, can be viewed in the cultural, political and economic spheres of the group. But one cannot propose a stagnant web of inter-relationships, which evolved between various groups as if there were no specific historical changes, or that the Kathkari identity was a fixed and homogeneous one. It may be difficult to actually provide instances of this except for the colonial period for which records are available.

Thus there are references to the migration of the Kathkaris from Gujarat to their present day position in the Konkan coastal region of Maharashtra, the interaction with African slaves in the 16th century, the adoption of, or evolving a specific dialect of Marathi, marriages with lower-caste non-Kathkari groups, the giving up of beef by a large number of Kathkaris and of course the complex repercussions of colonialism during which land ownership became an important resource for livelihood. Such a dynamic historical perspective is important to prevent a perception of a static Kathkari identity.

Heterogeneous Identity

Fourthly, we are aware of the oversimplification involved in talking of a Kathkari identity as if it is clearly homogeneous. There are differences within the Kathkaris which may have been the result of specific historical incidents like the conversion of some to Christianity or Islam, due to intercaste marriages or through the process of taking on cultural traits of settled Hindu communities due to prolonged contact, especially in the context of the division created due to a taboo on beef-eating groups.

But on the other hand in spite of all this, as the term Kathkari was clearly used to identify these groups, from within and without, it is not a fallacy to talk of a Kathkari identity, provided we view it as an open-ended and changing one, often responding to socio-political environments. The fact that Kathkaris live in small settlements dispersed throughout the district does explain the differences existing among them as each settlement developed peculiarities specific to its location thus adding to the heterogeneity of the community.

Nomadic Life

Finally, an obvious and important point, that their nomadic way of life had played an important role in giving them a particular identity in the region, and probably has contributed to their capacity to change and adapt to newer cultural and economic environments. This is an important aspect in the history of the Kathkaris, enabling them to respond in critical ways to new situations, rarely showing a rigidity in their approach. However, we have avoided a tendency to talk of a "glorious past" of the Kathkari or any attempts at portraying them as a one-dimensional indigenous group with an exclusive identity.

Myths of Origins.

Tracing their origins in their myth, Gisbert writes, "The Kathkaris of Poona... think that they descend from the monkey",[53] an idea reflected quite often in Kathkari folklore. Walt also mentions their story that "they are descended from the monkeys which the god Ram took with him against the demon king of Ceylon (now Sri Lanka)".[54] This myth embodies the idea that they are an indigenous group to the region, even as they may have actually changed their locations over a period of time, making it possible for them to see their ancestral linkage to the forests with their forefathers being the original inhabitants, having descended from the monkeys themselves.

Environmental Links

This links them up to the region in a way that ensures a certain belonging even as they may move in vast tracts of land. Thus, being indigenous as reflected in the myth does not limit their tendency to migrate as the forests act as a continuity in different areas, ensuring a sense of belonging.

A number of the documents under survey indicate that the Kathkaris may have arrived in the present region of Maharashtra from the north, specifically from central and southern Gujarat. If this movement did take place, then their myth of origin can be seen to give them a sense of belonging to their familiar environment, i.e. the forests, in a new geographical area. The myth can be meaningful in any area from Gujarat to Maharashtra, both of which are recent political boundaries, provided the environment acts as a resource in familiar ways.

The identification with the monkeys which aided Ram in his fight against Ravana, reveals the influence of mainstream Hinduism, symbolizing a long term contact with neighbouring settled cultivator groups. It also marks a distinction which was maintained, as the group identified with as not from mainstream society but from the forest, the monkeys who helped Ram, implying neither isolation from other groups nor complete integration.

As further analysis will reveal the forests played an important role in their economic and cultural lives providing alternative occupations even when they maintained exchange relations with other groups of the region. Thus in their myths one constantly sees the influence of symbols identified as Hindu which do not, however, imply that their religious system could be labelled as Hinduism.

In this regard we can look at the Kathkaris from the point of view of the neighbouring settled societies who saw them as marginals, as a people of the forest who may be primitive in their beliefs and practices and are different from the settled population. And if they do not have traditional and obligatory relations of economic exchange which is important for caste relations, these are to a certain extent, not part of their social world.

Inter-group Relationships

As the analysis of the economic systems of the Kathkaris will reveal, the absence of such obligations enabled a strong distinction between them and other groups. The Kathkaris in turn would view the others as people of the region with whom they have some exchange relations, which exist at the cultural as well as economic level, but who are necessarily different, because their existence in the forests implies a non-dependence on other groups and so an escape from obligatory relations.

The Bombay Gazetteer[55] gives a list of the variety of trees in the forests of the region. Trees yielding timber to be used in the making of plough and houses, toddy yielding trees, those with medicinal value and the Khair, which yields kath, are only some of those mentioned, revealing the enormous potential of the forests to sustain self-sufficiency among its inhabitants.

Ribas surmises that they "are probably of Bhil origin and are believed to have come from the north and to have originally settled in the Gujarat Athavisi, the present district of Surat".[56] Walt's understanding that they "are believed to have entered the district of Thana from the North",[57] goes on to match Ribas' statement and is repeated by Zimmermann.[58] Vyas summarizes the various arguments on the thesis and indicates the difficulty in getting a definite picture, which could be related to the observation that the Kathkari identity is a heterogeneous and an open-ended one. Thus he cites different scholars referring to the community as "a sub-section of the Bhils", as "Dravidian" and eventually as indicating a "considerable inter-mixture".[59]

Our emphasis will be on the heterogeneity within the Kathkaris in terms of some physical, cultural and economic differences, which seems to indicate an open-ended identity intrinsic to their history.

Occupational Diversity

Variety and Specialization

The Kathkaris have been doing a wide variety of activities for their livelihood. Cultivation, collecting and selling forest produce, rearing goats and hens, tapping forest palms, hunting and working as field labourers.[60] This does not include the additional work done by women in the domestic sphere. Their name though, has been derived from the word "katha" or catechu, an important ingredient in "paan", the extraction of which gave them an identity *vis-a-vis* their neighbouring ethnic groups.

It may, however not necessarily be a name originating in the group as has happened with a number of tribes whose terms for themselves tallied with their word for 'human-being' distinguishing themselves from other species of the natural environment. The fact that most documents written on them at the turn of the century use the term Kathkari indicates that the name was most commonly used, sometimes along with a variant, 'Kathodi'.

That the term Kathkari symbolizes a meaningful relationship of exchange with other groups reveals a move towards specialization which is characteristic of the castes of the region like the Kunbis and Agris who had taken to settled cultivation many years before. The

Kathkaris, as they are presented in historical and anthropological records, were nomadic, not owning land or having a fixed sedentary profession,[61] but at the same time having some exchange relations with other groups. Mostly for salt and oil given in exchange for some forest produce or labour. It is difficult to say that catechu-making was their primary occupation even though they may have specialized in it.

Organic Links

They still were organically linked to the forests, which provided for a diversity of alternative occupations. Though they may have also worked as labourers on the fields of other more settled groups, their dependence on this as a sole means of survival has not been a consistent part of their history. And it can also be said that "catechu" making could not have been a basis for a day-to-day exchange relation with neighbouring groups as the need for the product was felt by more specialized agencies who were part of a wider economic system.

Walt discusses the history of the product and states that it was exported from India as early as the 16th century and extracted chiefly in Surat, Malabar, Bengal and ceylon (now Sri Lanka). It could have been exchanged for goods or money and the extraction-production would be done only for about three to four months in a year. This meant resorting to other activities for the remaining period, again provided by the forests. Unlike the Thakkurs who were traditional toddy tappers in the area having sustained interaction with settled societies, the Kathkaris could still be fairly independent of the outside world.

Their links to the forests did not mean that they were an isolated group but only implies a diversity of occupations which, accompanied by their nomadism, helped in maintaining an autonomous ethnic identity. But just as their myth of origins which signified their indigenous nature without excluding possibilities of migration, the existence of a Kathkari identity did not signify a fixed unchanging cultural boundary nor did it exclude possibilities of change and inclusion of other groups into its fold.

Subdivisions

The divisions within the Kathkaris, which Ribas mentions as "Athavas, Dheds, Siddhis, Sons and Varaps", supports this vision of cultural change as each of these supposed divisions can be viewed in specific contexts responding to certain historical circumstances.

Ribas presents them as if they are intrinsic divisions within the

Kathkari fold:

> The Sons do not eat beef and are allowed to draw water at the village well and to enter the Kunbis houses and temples. The Sidhis are unmistakably of African origin, and are probably the descendants of Kathkari women and Negro immigrants. The Varaps or reverts may have been either Christians or Muslims formerly. The Dhors or Dheds are beef-eaters and therefore the lowest of the tribe socially.[62]

Only Zimmerman mentions the Athavas and links this endogenous group to the Gujarat Athavisi, at present a district of Surat,[63] but no details are provided by other sources either.

Sons and Dhors

This passage can be alternatively read in a way that sees each of these categories as responses to specific instances in Kathkari history. Out of the five divisions mentioned by Ribas, others like, Vyas,[64] Walt,[65] Weling,[66] and Zimmermann[67] feel that only two i.e. Sons and Dhors seem to have a basis in social organization. But as Weling points out even this division has a historical basis:

> . . . the Kathkaris, once a primitive aboriginal tribe had no compunction to eat beef. At the rise of neo-Brahmanism after the decay of Buddhism, the patronage to the cow as the specially sacred animal of the Brahmins was extended and beef-eating for the Hindus was rigidly prohibited.[68]

This may have influenced a large number of Kathkaris who interacted with communities which prohibited beef, and who then came to comprise Son Kathkaris, distinguishing themselves from the relatively isolated members who then comprised the Dhors. But the Sons did not take on a lifestyle which tallied with upper-caste Hindus and their diet continued to include animals like monkeys, rats, porcupines and squirrels which remained alien to other communities.[69] By giving up beef-eating they did not necessarily become affiliated to Hinduized groups, but accepting the taboo meant being accepted as exchange partners by them or even as labourers without pollution taboos.

The fact that marriages between Sons and Dhors came to be prohibited implied a conscious distancing on the part of the former, implying their increasing dependence on neighbouring groups, while the Dhors may have been comparatively self-sufficient even though it may have been difficult to continue being so. The small number of the Dhors present today is testimony to this.

The giving up of beef seemed to have a symbolic intention as it allowed for interaction for economic purposes, even as we see them as inextricably linked to motives of status for the community. The symbolic intention is supported by the fact that the people, as mentioned earlier, continued with a diet not shared by caste-Hindus, but which nevertheless did not have a religious sanction against it, making way for a fascinating co-existence which maintained cultural autonomy and permitted exchange relationships.

Varaps and Siddhis

The other three 'divisions' can be seen as indicators of an inclusive Kathkari identity wherein social exchange with other groups got fused. The Varaps and Siddhis are also very few in number and Weling mentions that he never came across any during his fieldwork.[70] The Varaps may have reverted from their converted status during a particular period. There is evidence of individuals even from lower-caste neighbouring communities having married into the Kathkari community. For these, reverting back may not have been very difficult at any point of time. As far as Christian conversion is concerned there is evidence to show that they were a very tiny group, and many would simply go back to the forests. For conversion demanded a reorientation of a worldview accompanied by a different eco-political subculture, in the absence of which it was difficult to sustain. Seen historically, the Varaps were part of this conflict of subcultures but there is little indication that they comprised a separate endogamous group.

Regarding the Siddhis, Weling writes that they "are Kathkaris so distinguished because of their admixture with the Siddhi, the Abyssinian negro of Janjira" *(ibid.,)*. In the *Bombay Gazetteer,* Vol. XI, on Kolaba and Janjira, J. M. Campbell discusses the rise of the Siddhis, an important naval force in the Konkan region, from being slaves and servants of the Portuguese, to becoming an important aristocratic group of the region in the seventeenth century. Intermarriages with native groups are also mentioned, and the author acknowledges the presence of a distinct subgroup among the Kathkaris called Siddhis. Gisbert narrates an incident where one member tried to "convince my reluctant self that pygmies were their immediate ancestors",[71] and the Kathkari expression he quotes is "small negroes with big paunches". It would have been helpful if Gisbert had given the exact Marathi word the Kathkari had used.

This thesis does have a lot of scholarly supporters. For example, Prof. Pravin Patkar of the Tata Institute of Social Sciences, Bombay[72] talks of the origins of the Kathkaris themselves as linked to the interaction between African slaves brought by the Jauhar Siddhi, a strong naval power in the 16th century on the western coast, and a local aboriginal tribe. However, it is not clear whether this local community was the "original" Kathkari one or whether the consequent interaction gave rise to such an identity.

These questions though, are unimportant and quite futile for our purpose here. For it is difficult to trace actual origins of identity as one inevitably comes across cases of fusion and change.

Distinctive Culture

What a theory of origins does do is throw up the possibility of viewing the history of the group as a relatively distinct cultural entity, which could have formed as a response to specific economic forces and historical processes of the region, growing not out of isolation but as part of a larger evolution. As Walt mentions that the export of catechu from Surat took place in as early as the 16th century, it is likely that communities closer to forests would be chosen to undertake this task, by special agencies, a move linked to the formation of the Kathkari identity.

Adaptive Exchange

In this context it would be pertinent to take a look at Weling's hypothesis:

> I am led to believe that Kathkaris are not a distinct tribal race, as the surnames suggest different tribes and castes of the Bombay presidency must have been mixed among the Kathkaris, and the possible old pre-dravidian stock has disappeared now beyond recognition. Members from castes following a totemistic organization might have brought their totems along with them and the traces found are due to their admission. My hypothesis is supported by the accounts of Mackintosh, Wilson and others, from which it is clear that the Kathkaris used to admit or force young men from the surrounding lower hindu castes and other tribes into their fold. The youth who married Kathkari women and lived with

them were excommunicated by the people of their former castes.[73]

Weling's observation is supported by Zimmermann who, though in a different context, observes that there were intermarriages with Konkan girls, which he feels points to the possibility that Kathkaris in Khandala immigrated from the Konkan.[74]

If Weling's hypothesis is true, it implies that boys from different communities, especially lower caste groups, would marry into the Kathkari settlement bringing some of their earlier cultural traits along and contributing to the heterogeneity of a changing identity. One can only speculate about the reason why such marriages took place. It is very possible that these youth could have perceived the Kathkaris as a more attractive alternative to the caste discrimination they could not have otherwise escaped. Such marriages become agencies for introducing Hinduized customs in a consequent two way exchange.

Unlike the theory of imitation, this process implies that the "non-Kathkari" youth also had to adapt himself to a different culture, by the very act of marrying into these tribal settlements. Conversely though, one can also see greater similarities between lower-castes and the lowly tribals making such marriages easier for both though they may have resulted in ostracism and excommunication by the other castes.

Kathkari Identity

From this discussion we can conclude that the Kathkari identity is an open-ended and inclusive one, based on a food-gathering culture and variously related occupations linked to the local economy and markets, allowing for a wide range of ways for earning a livelihood. This is most apparent and best documented for when colonialism began to intrude into their world, but it can simultaneously be seen as an indication of their means of responding to change even in the past. It is not unreasonable to assume that their adaptive response to changes precipitated by colonialism were modelled on other such adaptations in their earlier history.

It would be important to now discuss some characteristics of the community in terms of language, political and gender relations, even as we are aware that they are not separate spheres but only concepts having an analytical use.

Tribal Dialects

Regarding their language there are a number of theories, some of which refer to it as a dialect of Marathi, labelling it as a "corrupt" form.[75] To others it shows traces of a hint of Gujarati, and still others believe that it changed from a language which was peculiar to the community to one which was strongly influenced by the local language.[76] Such different theories continue to be debated even today and underscore the twofold difficulty: either tracing the origins of a distinctive Kathkari language, or conversely, claiming that their language is a dialect of Marathi with no peculiarities of its own.

Distinct and Adapted

Vyas points out that in Rajasthan the Kathkaris "have developed a new dialect which is a combination of Vagdi and Marathi",[77] strengthening the view that the linguistic identity of the people is strongly linked to other aspects of socio-economic relations. The Kathkaris may have had a language different from either Marathi or Gujarati at some point of time. Ribas traces the existence of some words to those found among the Bhils,[78] a thesis also supported by Weling who feels that originally the Kathkari language was linked to a Bhil dialect, Khandeshi.[79] But in response to different needs arising from migration they adapted to local dialects, explaining why their language in Raigad is unmistakably a dialect of Marathi even if a bit different.

This adaptation to local neighbourhoods is acknowledged also by Zimmermann when he points out that there are differences in usage even within the community among those living in different areas like "Thana, Janjira and Kolaba".[80] He also traces the original dialect to Khandeshi[81] and discusses their tendency to "shorten words by dropping inflectional endings",[82] a feature also mentioned by Walt who is convinced that they have no peculiar language of their own and tend to "reduce words and shorten speech, and uniformly endeavor to get rid of the personal, not the tense, inflections of the verbs".[83]

A picture of a complex use of language which finally emerges, shows the connection of language to changing situations where the Kathkaris, like any other human group, have shown a dynamism and responsiveness which reveals their capacity to adapt and change.

A number of scholars studying communities like the Kathkaris have acknowledged a sophisticated use of communication, where often the tribals amongst themselves speak a language quite different from the one they employ when interacting with other groups around. A fact also mentioned by Weling.[84] Such a bilingualism which is intrinsic to their communication further supports the notion of exchange as being as much a part of Kathkari identity, as it is of other groups.

Social Organization

Gisbert, during his fieldwork amongst the community "once asked a Kathkari notable whether there was any memory of a great man of his tribe",[85] and was surprised to get a negative answer making him state that "myth and traditions have failed to provide them with heroes, whose real existence in most cases is problematic. . . .".[86] But this observation may precisely be linked to the lack of information and focus on the political aspects of the community. In fact Weling in his thesis, makes very little mention of the political organization of the community, either in relation to wider political processes or at the level of the specific settlement.

Zimmermann refers to the political organization of the Kathkaris as "a constitutional monarchy with a somewhat strong emphasis on the democratic element".[87] The headman, or chief takes the initiative in settling disputes within the settlement, but if the case requires a meeting with the leaders of other communities then an appeal may be made to a tribal assembly. Aspects of their political life may have undergone a lot of change in response to historical factors, but certain stable factors can always be noticed. For example the existence of certain roles within the settlement meant for the chief, the bhagat, the bua and the dhaulari.

Specific Roles

While the chief acts as a representative of the people and a kind of judge during disputes, the bhagat wields his, and occasionally her, influence as the medicineman/woman in touch with the supernatural. The bua is some kind of a religious person, initiated by a guru from a neighbouring caste, and who abstains from drink and non-vegetarian food, while the dhaulari is an elderly lady playing the official role during marriage ceremonies.

Though these are discernible roles with separate spheres of influence, they comprise a set of people who may collectively influence decisions related to the settlement and may even substitute each other, as when the headman takes on the role of the bua or dhaulari[88] or when the bua takes on the role of the chief if the latter is seen as incapable. Weling observes that the 'naik-ship' is not a hereditary one, though if the grown up son is efficient he may succeed his father. This open-endedness probably makes it easy for another person to take on the naik's role in case he is seen as unworthy.

It is difficult to say whether each of the four positions have had the same influence throughout their history, as there is not enough material on this aspect. Yet, one can somewhat confidently say that different situations may have seen the rise of a particular position at some specific time.

For example, the role of the bua may have either arisen or may have gained importance when exchange relations with other communities had a greater significance in their life. Thus the token approval of the values of non-drinking and vegetarianism. The dhaulari seems to have lost her importance as upper-castes became significant reference groups for the Kathkaris and a brahmin priest substituted her role. As the British "sarcar", began having an overwhelming presence in their life the naik's role in representing his people became very pertinent, especially when some residents of the Kathwadi, i.e. the Kathkari hamlet in the village, were "suspected as perpetrators of crime or mischief".[89]

Sagas and Legends

In the stories of the Kathkari, there are references made to kings and even a version of the *Ramayana* is mentioned.[90] Most of such stories refer to palace intrigues and conflicts over lineages. This awareness of political processes on a different scale than their own once again reveals their contact with neighbouring communities. Weling traces the origin of most of their stories to material picked up from "the Gondhalis and Powadewallas, a class of professional story tellers and bards of the Deccan who in their turn had based the stories on popular Hindu mythology and history".[91] Such sagas of kings reflected political problems quite different from the everyday life of their own situation, even though it implied seeing themselves as part of a larger scenario.

On the other hand another legend which is based on a Kathkari chief's life, revolves around the hunting and cooking of a hare, and its subsequent theft from the soup pot by the chief's sons, who are then duly punished.[92] The chief leads a life like any other member of the community and his concerns are not any different. The delegation of duties in terms of political needs are of a different kind altogether and have to be seen in their own functional context. Perhaps it is for this reason that there is not much attention paid to this aspect in most of the documents on the Kathkaris, though one can see why Zimmermann referred to their political organization as having a strong emphasis on democracy.

Gender Relations

Role Allocations

It is possible to get an idea of the gender relations within the community, from observations made on the economic, social and religious systems of the community. Women have played an equal role in the economic life besides the domestic sphere, and food-gathering, fishing and collection of forest produce has been as much their work as that of the men. Even in the work of catechu-making, Walt mentions a division of labour on the basis of gender, where both men and women did different but complementary tasks.[93]

Thus any understanding of a Kathkari identity must visualize the contribution of both the sexes in the existence of the community. There was division of labour based on sex, and work at home was largely confined to the woman, while hunting was a task reserved for the men. But it must be remembered that most of the food supplies for the daily living was dependent more on food-gathering and exchange, than on hunting. So even with the division of labour, women were as much part of the public space as the domestic one.

There is, though, no mention of a woman chief, but the dhaulari, who played an important role in marriage ceremonies acted as a symbol of women in the public space, even though her importance has gradually decreased.

Marriage Customs

The institution of marriage, among the Kathkaris, has all the stability which one expects in more settled societies and it is mentioned quite often that violation of marital relations is seen as a serious crime.

> Concrete instances that prove the prevailing fidelity both on the part of the husband and wife are not wanting. A mere aspersion to the contrary may drive a Kathkari into the jungle to hide himself.[94]

Gisbert also mentions the importance given to "conjugal fidelity",[95] which at the same time acknowledges that the threat to this fidelity is very real. In fact there is reason to believe that Kathkari women had less restrictions on their desires and demands, in comparison to neighbouring communities like the Kunbis and Agris.

If the girl's parents could not find a husband for their daughter, she had to go "and seek one for herself among her friends. When she has found one, she returns home by herself, and her husband-to-be follows her in a few days".[96] He also mentions a case when a widow wanted to live with a man who had deserted his wife, and her settlement members eventually allowed them to live together. Weling gives the example of a widow, aged 42, who was the richest woman in the Kathwadi, the outcome of the "joint labour" of her late husband and her. She attracted a widower two years her younger and got married to him "irrespective of the common ridicule".[97]

The custom of bride-price required the boys' side to undergo considerable expenditure for a marriage, and divorces and desertions were also common. A woman could leave her husband and, even though she was not allowed to remarry while he was alive, she could live with someone else. The man on the other hand, could divorce his wife and remarry as many times as he wished, and could also keep more than one wife. The patrilocal set up is usual, but there are exceptional cases where the husband has left his house and lived with his wife.[98]

Division of Labour

The division of labour between the sexes does not by itself signify an unequal relation and women have been a part of both the public and private space. But the existence of different rules and regulations for women does indicate male domination in certain spheres, especially that of political organization. But there is a wide variety of responses to specific situations. If certain labels like, 'patrilocal' or 'patrilineal' can be used for their marriage customs there is still a lot of deviation which takes place making any clear cut categorization problematic.

Dependency Development

Early Responses

Weling, writing during the early decades of this century presents a picture of the Kathkaris very different from the pessimistic one so prevalent today. He was writing at a time when forests had already been encroached upon by governmental agencies. The Kathkari's

> services are in demand everywhere. The landlords want him as his labour is comparatively cheaper than that of the Kunbi as he can put in more work with lesser wages. Perhaps it is

> for the same reason that contractors and traders in coal, wood, roadmaking, etc., want Kathkari labour. And as long as he can answer satisfactorily this belief of the capitalists or land lords in his skill, working capability and cheapness of labour, he has an advantage in the struggle for existence over many other village castes. Wherever I found the Kathkari I found him in a comparatively prosperous condition. It is certain that all through the year he manages to support himself and his family.[99]

This picture did undergo a drastic change in subsequent years and was anyway not representative of the major part of their population. But it does go a long way in challenging the priori generalizations on the Kathkaris and contradicts the negative stereotypes built around them. It proves that the community was able to respond on its own to the complex forces of colonialism, even though the world was becoming more and more incomprehensible to them.

Gradual Decline

Zimmermann begins his essay on the Kathkaris written in the year 1921, with the following passage:

> They emerge from the ravines round about, carrying small quantities of toddy, firewood, wild mangoes, fish or berries. Timidly they offer their wares for sale, coming and going without greeting. If they succeed in disposing off what they had brought, they will go straight to a shop to buy provisions for their families, such as rice, nachni, chillies, dhal, salt and other necessaries for a jungle household. Any money left over will be spent on ornaments. Others still less thrifty get rid of their money in the liquor shop, drinking without restraint, whereupon they will be seen staggering and quarrelling along the road.[100]

This passage reveals the continuity in their exchange relationship with neighbouring groups, but in a new context. The scene described is that of a *bazaar* in Khandalla and symbolizes the existence of a monetary economy in to which the Kathkaris seem to be well assimilated. They sell a wide variety of forest produce, indicative of a food-gathering economy. Their money is used for buying goods from a different mode of production, settled cultivation. Ornaments and liquor too represent an integration into the monetary economy, especially the latter which tells a complex story of centralization of the economy with the presence of the British government and commercial use of forest produce, as has been mentioned earlier. Gradually, the Kathkaris become more and more dependent on labour in exchange for money as a means of livelihood, since they have no land assets.

By the time Zimmermann was writing, this process had already been introduced:

> A good many members of these tribes have left off catechu making, their original occupation. They now find labour as rice cleaners and workers in the fields for two or three months of the year. A few support themselves by tilling poorer varkas soil.[101]

The importance of this point is to stress the constant change and adaptation, through which the Kathkaris were going. The community had kept its cultural and economic autonomy along with keeping its exchange relations with other groups following a different mode of production, but found itself slowly getting integrated into a centralized economy, through the colonial intervention, and in a position of extreme dependence, forcing them into an unequal exchange.

Dependency and Degradation

Colonialism changed things drastically for the Kathkaris like it did for all other communities. Earlier their life was intimately linked to their forests. This did not imply isolation, but provided for an alternative to dependence on labour or local markets as their sole means of survival. When the forests began being put to government sponsored commercial use, first for wood to be used in shipbuilding and subsequently for the railways, this means of livelihood was usurped and the tribals were made dependent on their wage labour for survival.

Thus Campbell writing in 1870, in his list of the flora of the region[102] mentions how the number of Dhavda trees was drastically reduced due to over-exploitation as its wood was required for railway sleepers. Of course, local officials were often bribed by the tribals to allow them to use the forests, an exchange which goes on to this day, but the signals were now clear. The forests could no longer be used by the Kathkaris on their own terms for their traditional purposes.

Their diversity of occupations was now drastically narrowed, even as their need for wage-labour increased. But it was not easy to introduce the Kathkaris to use money in a system of commercial exchange, however urgent this may have been for a government in a hurry to rationalize a traditional tribal economy for its own needs. Liquor became a perverse means of doing this, through the banning of traditional toddy tapping and restricting the sale of distilled liquor to licensed manufacturers.

Toddy consumption, a traditional part of Kathkari culture, changed its significance drastically. Instead of being able to meet their needs from an exchange with the traditional toddy tappers like the Thakkurs and Agris, they were now led to buy distilled liquor from specialized centres, drawing them further into the monetary economy. Thus their fate to work as wage labourers was sealed, tying them firmly into an unequal economic exchange with an ever increasing one way dependence.

Another example of such a dependency leading to their degradation is in the case of those Kathkaris who migrated to Rajasthan from Maharashtra. "They were brought to Rajasthan by Bohra Forest contractors to work as forest labourers for making katha from Kher trees."[103] He goes on to elaborate their case. Earlier, only the males came but were later on joined by their families and when Vyas was doing his research, they could be found in Shahabad tehsil of Kota district and villages of Udaipur district:

> The condition of the Kathodis in the Kher forests became worse when the forest was denuded. This involved the Kathodis in a struggle for existence...Their standard of living is below the subsistence level. When they began to starve they decided to go back to their native place in Maharashtra. They moved towards their native place and in the process some of them separated and settled down in the other villages. Some of them were seen starving to death near Rishabhdeo town, forty miles south of Udaipur.[104]

This grim picture shows how the new system of economic exchange created negative conditions for those members who had taken the initiative to come so far away from their territory. Though they were doing the familiar work of katha extraction, their employers could not absorb them into alternative occupations.

During their stay in Rajasthan, as can be seen from the life of those who lived on, they continued to adapt to new situations. Vyas in his study of their clan system points out that names of clans in Rajasthan differed from those in Maharashtra, because after they were culturally cut off from their earlier community, they gave up their original clan names and adopted new ones.[105] Secondly, he asserts, "there are many clans which are the same as those of the Bhils of the area around".[106] He goes on to say that the clans were of different kinds, while some names were totemistic, others were territorial and some others referred to professions. Another significant example of their adaption was the development of a new dialect, a combination of Vagadi and Marathi.

The whole dimension of clan names is important as it symbolizes the changes the tribal group is undergoing, especially as they adapt to newer environments. In fact it is an inquiry into clan names that made Weling curious about their patterns of endo/exogamy leading to his hypothesis on the heterogeneity of Kathkari culture.

Mission Contact

The Jesuit missionaries contact with the Kathkaris began in 1894. While the influence of the mission did go a long way in helping them adjust to changes, the Kathkaris were by no means passive recipients of such action. Conversions to Christianity, more often than not were seen as superficial even by the mission, dubbing them "rice Christians". Difficulties in making them see the relevance of "education" often lead to frustration among the missionaries and this was projected on the perceived "faults" within this community. Very little empathy seemed to exist towards the community's way of life which was clearly seen as undesirable, as the discussion on the literature produced by the mission has shown.

Gisbert though, leaves images of the Kathkari in new occupations, during his visit to the Kune mission: " A young Kathkari supplying medicines to a mother as he instructs her how to administer them to her young child, a boy on a sewing machine, and another on a bench-vice".[107] In fact Ribas' report mentions a large number of new activities which involved the Kathkaris, from candle and lace production to weaving and technical training.[108] But the number of those in contact with the mission were, a tiny fragment of the entire Kathkari population. And even those associated with the mission were not really able to break their dependencies as the report reveals.[109]

However those few Kathkaris who were allotted land in their name, managed to adapt themselves to the changes brought by colonialism independently of any help from the mission. Indeed, wherever the Kathkaris have been provided alternatives to forest resources and a chance to escape dependence as labourers, though instances of these are far fewer than they ought to be, these tribals have been able to make the same breakthrough to development in their situation, just as other communities have.

Contemporary Awakenings

Land Recovery

Earlier, wherever the community practiced agriculture it was in the form of shifting cultivation which was viewed by the British as encroachments. The land was owned collectively and the representative of the land was the chief of that particular settlement. In 1957 the state government gave land ownership rights to all tillers by getting the tenancy law amended, but even this did not prevent tribals from being tricked into selling their land for a pittance or transferring their land. It was only in 1974 that legislation was passed in their favour, preventing land alienation among the tribals through the Maharashtra Restoration of Lands to Scheduled Tribes Act 1974.[110]

This legally enabled the adivasis to buy back the land that was validly transferred by them to others between April 1957 and July 1974 and the Maharashtra Land Revenue Code and Tenancy Laws Amendment Act entitled them to get back free the land that was illegally transferred.[111] It was decided to regularize land in their favour and give it to individual land owners. The land was to be taken away from the forest department and given to the revenue department, so that its distribution for the tribals could be done easily.

Unfortunately, this was never completed, as the excess power given to the local collectors and the consequent corruption by the government officials acted as obstacles to this process. Vohra analyses in detail some of the other reasons why it was never done.[112] The inability of the tribals to comprehend the importance of getting the land back in their name is seen by him as a major obstacle. According to academic-activist Pravin Patkar, even though seventy per cent of the relevant land was given to the revenue department, most of these cases were sealed and filed away by the officials who usurped the land.[113] Patkar's statement has been validated by a number of journalistic investigations.

In the *Indian Express,* Bombay edition dated 24th October 1992, Pramod Pagedar accused Maharashtra Finance Minister Ram Rao Adik and his relations of buying large tracts of *adivasi* and *dalit* land in Thane and Raigad District in contravention of the law that forbids such sale and purchase. Another report of a similar kind had appeared in the same newspaper on 2nd August 1992, which reported the land grabbing scam unearthed by Thane district collector Madhukar Patil, in which the names of businessmen from Bombay were also mentioned. According to this report the staff and officials of the Revenue Department of the district had a major role to play. These officials were also implicated by a report in *The Daily,* a Bombay newspaper, on 29th December 1992.

There have been a few cases where certain settlements did get the land transferred on to their names, and these have been the result of the pressure of agencies and movements like the Bhoodan Andolan. But by and large, there have not been many examples of political mobilization or pressure groups which could take up the *dali* land issue in its agenda. The last fifteen years or so, though, have seen some voluntary agencies fighting on behalf of the Kathkaris, on various issues.

The Yusuf Meherally Centre, which has a programme in Tara village of Raigad district has, under the leadership of Surekha Dalvi, a sustained programme to have the land transferred in the name of the individuals within the community.[114] Parivartan '84, under the leadership of Prof. Pravin Patkar had made a number of concrete efforts to implement the welfare measures for the tribals, and this organization was instrumental in having the exploitative practice of charcoal-making banned by the state government, even though the officials were unsuccessful in providing alternative employment for the adivasis.[115] In Raigad district alone, there are around thirteen voluntary organizations[116] many of which are involved with Kathkaris in the region.

Political Involvement

Morchas and demonstrations have found the Kathkaris responding in large numbers, signalling their readiness to speak the political language of the times. Such a language is an important one as the region is undergoing drastic changes, affecting the Kathkaris in a big way. The vision of progress and development which the government has, does not include the tribals, and more often than not, they find themselves impoverished and dependent within a landscape which has all the symbols of a prosperous economic scenario, e.g., big industries, dams and luxurious hotels,etc..

Gautam Vohra, who heads the Development Research and Action Group in Pen Taluka of Raigad District, a mentions in a report in the *Indian Express,* Bombay, dated 6th July 1992, of two such projects and their negative effects on the tribals of the region. The Hetovane Dam project, to provide water for citizens of New Bombay, is due for completion in 1998. It has been erected on the Bhogeshwari river which is an important source of water for local inhabitants during the dry season and which now cannot provide the required amount of water due to the dam construction, which was also responsible for the felling of trees in the area. The Mahal Mira Hill Resort forced many tribals to sell off their land because the link road, connecting the Pen-Khopoli Road, passed through their properties.

Conclusion

Resources Available

As of now, we can conclude this chapter by restating the argument made throughout this presentation, that the Kathkaris are no exception to the dynamism of human groups and their capacity to adapt to changing times. They are as much products of history as all of us, and if they have found themselves as victims of circumstances it is not because they have "inherent" characteristics which make such a subordination possible, so much as the existence of processes and agencies which force unequal exchange relationships onto them. Their history has to be seen as linked to such wider processes. If we do, however, find a perception of this community as a regressive and passive group, it is more a testimony to the weaknesses and limitations of the documentation on the community rather than an accurate reflection of the people themselves, and their intrinsic character.

For our reconstruction of the Kathkaris' profile demonstrates that they were a sufficiently diverse and heterogeneous group to find within their tribe the necessary cultural and economic resources to adapt themselves to their changing historical situations.

Unequal Exchange

It is only with the colonial penetration of their traditional habitats that they lose all control over the terms of exchange between themselves and the outside world. And as this exchange becomes increasingly unfair and unsympathetic to the people, the economic viability of their tribal way of life, and their positive self-image that sustained it, both collapse, and together with this they lose their ability to adapt and preserve their distinctiveness and self-appreciation, even as they had done all through their earlier history. Moreover, there is now no space left for them to withdraw into, geographically or otherwise.

Alternative Approaches

The changes that began with the colonial era and have intensified with the development which followed have brought them little else but a denial of their human dignity and a negation of their tribal culture. A benevolent paternalism, that characterized the missionary encounter with them, and which found a place in the colonial administration as well, still continues in the tribal sub-plans of today. But these interventions are grossly inadequate and unfortunately rather misplaced in the face of the enormous tragedy that has been perpetrated on these Kathkaris.

For all these initiatives treat them as 'passive objects' of another's benevolence. But, if their history tells us anything, it is that the Kathkaris will only be able to regain their dignity and reconstruct their identity, in the measure in which they become once again 'active subjects' of their history, recreators of the culture and equal partners in their economic exchanges; rather than abject sufferers of the changes overtaking and overwhelming them at present.

This, indeed, is the lesson of their history as reconstituted here. For no way of life or culture can survive the destruction of the material basis on which it is built, and by which is sustained. Moreover, neither can a people be uplifted economically, or otherwise, and made self-reliant without a sustaining self-image which comes from a positive appreciation of their way of life, even as this must actively adapt and change to remain both distinctive and viable. Indeed, sustainable development for a people, must imply a sustainable way of life, and vice versa!

Hence, we must reconstitute a more equitable and dignified exchange relationship for these vulnerable people with the outside world that impinges on them so inexorably, only then will they be able to reconstruct their identity and regain their positive self-image. And just as their decline began with a deteriorating exchange relationship, their rehabilitation must also in turn begin with a reversal in this exchange as well.

REFERENCES

1. John Wilson, "Account of the Waralis and Katodis—two of The Forest-Tribes of northern Konkan", *Royal Asiatic Society of Great Britain and Ireland, Journal,* Vol. 7, Serial 13, 1843, pp.14-31.
2. *ibid.,* p.17.
3. *ibid.,* p. 30.
4. *ibid.,* p.26.
5. *ibid.*
6. *ibid.,* p. 30.
7. R. Zimmermann, *The Khandala Kathkaris,* British India Press, Mazagaon, Bombay, 1921. Sources include information from the missionaries in charge of the Kune settlement, *Bombay Gazetteer* Vol. XIII, *Bombay Census Report 1911,* Research

done by G. A. Grierson, M. Kennedy, and Sir Athelstane Baines besides the author's personal observations. (Cf. *ibid.*, p. 18).

8. *ibid.*, p. 5.
9. *ibid.*, p. 6.
10. *ibid.*, p. 17.
11. *ibid.*, p. 8.
12. *ibid.*, p. 7.
13. *ibid.*, p. 6.
14. *ibid.*, p. 7.
15. *ibid.*, p. 6.
16. *ibid.*
17. *ibid.*, p. 7.
18. *ibid.*
19. Cf. *ibid.*, p. 8.
20. *ibid.*, p. 8.
21. *ibid.*
22. *ibid.*
23. *ibid.*, p. 3.
24. *ibid.*, p. 5.
25. *ibid.*, p. 10.
26. *ibid.*, p. 17.
27. *ibid.*
28. *ibid.*
29. *ibid.*, p. 18.
30. Personal communication.
31. Unpublished typescript of the Social Welfare Centre, Kune, Khandala. PO. 412, Dist. Pune, Maharashtra.
32. A. Ribas "Socio-economic Survey of the Kune Mission—Part I", p. 16.
33. *ibid.*, p. 11.
34. *ibid.*, p. 16.
35. *ibid.*, p. 11.
36. *ibid.*
37. *ibid.*, p. 12.
38. *ibid.*
39. *ibid.*, p. 12.
40. *ibid.*
41. *ibid.*, p. 15.
42. *ibid.*
43. *ibid.*, p. 16.
44. *ibid.*, p. 16.
45. A. N. Weling, *The Kathkaris, a Sociological Study of an Aboriginal Tribe of the Bombay Presidency*, Bombay Book Depot, Girgaum, Bombay 1934. It was submitted to Dr. G.S. Ghurye of the School of Sociology and Economics of Bombay University as a Ph.D. Thesis.
46. Weling., p. 10 .
47. *ibid.*, emphasis added.
48. *ibid.*
49. *ibid.*, p. 150.
50. *ibid.*, p. 151.
51. *ibid.*, p. 34.
52. Cf. David Hardiman, *The Coming of the Devi: Adivasi Assertion in Western India*, Oxford University Press, Delhi, 1987.

53. Pascual Gisbert *Preliterate Man: A Synthetic View of Primitive Man,* Manaktalas, Bombay 1967, p. 239.
54. George Walt, *A Dictionary of Economic Products of India,* Cosmo, Bombay, 1972, p. 31.
55. *Bombay Gazetteer* Vol.XI., Kolaba and Janjira, p. 23.
56. Ribas, *op. cit.,* p. 6.
57. Walt, *op. cit.,* p. 31.
58. Zimmermann, *op. cit.,* p. 2.
59. Cf. N.N. Vyas, "Kathodi—A Tribe in Transition" in N. N. Vyas and R. S. Mann, eds., *Indian Tribes in Transition,* pp. 151-69.
60. J. M. Campbell, *Bombay Gazetteer,* Vol. XI, Kolaba and Janjira, 1870, p. 416.
61. *ibid.,* N. N. Vyas, *op.cit.,* p. 151.
62. Ribas, *op.cit.* pp.6-7.
63. Zimmerman, *op. cit.,* p.2.
64. Vyas, *op. cit.,* p. 153.
65. Walt, *op. cit.,* p. 31.
66. Weling, *op. cit.,* p. 51.
67. Zimmermann, *op. cit.,* p. 2.
68. Weling, *op. cit.,* p. 51.
69. Cf. J. Wilson, *op. cit.,* p.26.
70. Weling, *op. cit.,* p. 52.
71. Gisbert, *op. cit.,* p. 239.
72. personal communication.
73. Weling, *op. cit.,* pp. 54-5.
74. Zimmermann, *op. cit.,* p. 2.
75. Campbell, *op. cit.,* p. 416.
76. Weling, *op. cit.,* pp. 121-2.
77. Vyas, *op. cit.,* p. 156.
78. Ribas, *op. cit.,* p. 7.
79. Weling, *op. cit.,* p. 122.
80. Zimmermann, *op. cit.,* p. 4.
81. *ibid.*
82. *ibid.*
83. Walt, *op. cit.,* p. 31.
84. Weling, *op. cit.,* p. 121.
85. Gisbert, *op. cit.,* p. 2.
86. *ibid.*
87. Zimmermann, *op. cit.,* p. 10.
88. Zimmermann, *op. cit.,* p. 13 Weling, *op. cit.,* p. 62 and Campbell, *op. cit.,* p. 416.
89. Weling, *op. cit.,* p. 61.
90. Weling, *op. cit.,* p. 137.
91. *ibid.,* p. 133.
92. *ibid.,* pp. 142-3.
93. Walt, *op. cit.,* p. 32.
94. Zimmermann, *op. cit.,* p. 9.
95. Gisbert, *op. cit.,* p. 80.
96. Zimmermann, *op. cit.,* p. 9.
97. Weling, *op. cit.,* p. 71.
98. *ibid.,* p. 72.
99. Weling, *op. cit.,* p. 150.
100. Zimmermann, *op. cit.,* p. 1.
101. *ibid.,* p. 3.

102. Campbell, *op. cit.*, p. 23.
103. Vyas, *op. cit.*, p. 152.
104. *ibid.*, p. 153.
105. *ibid.*
106. *ibid.*
107. Gisbert, *op. cit.*, p. 252.
108. Ribas, *op. cit.*, pp. 19-20.
109. *ibid.*, p. 11.
110. *Maharashtra Act No. XIV of 1975*, published by the Maharashura Government, 1987.
111. Cf. Gautam Vohra, *Times of India*, Bombay-31.5.1976, cited in Vohra, *op. cit.*, p. 89.
112. *ibid.*
113. Personal communication.
114. Personal communication.
115. Personal communication.
116. Vohra, *op. cit.*, p. 10.

4

PERCEPTIONS OF IDENTITY AND DIGNITY

The previous chapter reconstructed the Kathkari profile from a critical analysis of the available sources. Here we turn to the data collected in the field to describe the Kathkaris' present situation, from the perceptions the various groups in the area interacting with them have of these people, as well as the self-perceptions of the Kathkaris themselves. The methodology used has been explained earlier in Chapter 2. Here the results are presented and analysed within the theoretical framework outlined in Chapter 1 and with the Kathkari profile, sketched in Chapter 3, in mind.

NON-KATHKARI PERCEPTIONS

Not unexpectedly the other communities in the neighbourhood viewed the Kathkaris according to the type of relationship they shared with them. Responses varied from indifference to condescension, reflecting the specific kind of interaction they had.

Dalits

Sangda

The people of a Sangda settlement of Baudhas, a local term for neo-Buddhists or dalits, who never really interacted with the Kathkaris on a day-to day basis, showed an unusual sympathy for them. This settlement is situated in Roha taluka and consists of six nuclear families affiliated to each other. Most work as labourers in villages closer to Roha town and a few go to the industrial area of Dhatao in the same taluka. The Kathkaris were viewed by them as a group which required special assistance by the government. Their economic backwardness was seen as being a result of forest denudation and land alienation, and it was suggested that they be given education whereby they learnt the value of saving.

More to the point, the Kathkaris were seen as being in the same position they themselves were some years ago. This perception is significant as it views the Kathkaris in a more historical light and also gives them the space to move out of their present state. They saw in the Kathkaris a bit of their own past, and as they felt that today they were in a much better position, the Kathkaris too would follow in the same direction, provided the required help was given.

The Kathkaris around this neo-Buddhist community lived about a couple of kilometers away and had very little interaction with them. Though, as both communities depended on labour as a means of survival, an element of competition could be expected, but was not actually detected. This may have been due to the fact that the neo-Buddhists went towards the town to look for work rather than the villages around, while the Kathkaris depended on agricultural labour. Hence they did not see each other as rivals. This seems all the more pertinent when we compare their experience with the same community of another settlement, Killa, in the same taluka.

Killa

The neo-Buddhists here, were literally pitted against the Kathkaris by the more dominant community in the area, the Marathas. The dominant position of the Marathas was due to their possession of land as well as their access to governmental agencies and by their general influence in the panchayat. Clearly, they were the dominant caste. The Kathkaris were living away from the Maratha village about a decade ago, as usual on a nearby hillock. The Marathas provided them with work in their fields and in this respect they competed with the neo-buddhists who were already living within the Maratha village, though on the outskirts.

The gram panchayat in the area was dominated by the Marathas and when they received funds to build houses for the Kathkaris, who are given special privileges by the government, they began asking the Kathkaris to come down and live in the village, but in the area presently inhabited by the neo-Buddhists. The Kathkaris came in small numbers throughout the last decade and their arrival was seen an encroachment by the dalit community. It is reported that there were a number of fights between the two subordinate groups and many of their rituals were perceived as being antagonistic. For example the neo-Buddhists practiced burial while the Kathkaris cremated the dead. Finally, the former group left and the entire Kathkari settlement came down to the Maratha village.

Thus the hostile relationship between the two communities in this case was very different from the one in Sangda, discussed earlier. But the evident control of the Marathas in this situation is obvious, and their attitude towards the Kathkaris reflects their own kind of interaction.

Here the tribals are a source of revenue to the Maratha village in the form of grants given in their name, but only when those in control manage to divert funds away from its real use. Thus the houses which were finally built for the Kathkaris were inevitably substandard, with most of the money taken away by intermediaries. A certain amount of confusion within the Kathkari settlement was also introduced when only some houses were made 'pucca', i.e. with bricks and mortar, at the instance of the gram panchayat, creating a lot of conflict between the members within the Kathkari community.

This dependence on the Marathas not only for work on the fields which is a long standing one, but also in other aspects of their now changing lives, created among both communities, their own peculiar ways of perceiving each other.

Marathas

Killa

The Marathas of Killa village, openly asserted that the Kathkaris were a good-for-nothing people, who were lazy drunkards. At the same time they could not deny their dependence on them for labour, a situation which had become more complex with an alternative work site for the Kathkaris in railway construction projects. We came across a Maratha woman cajoling a reluctant Kathkari to come to work, and at the same time telling us how lazy these people were and that they would never change. Even as interviews with the Kathkaris were in progress, a couple of Maratha men would stand within hearing distance, often interrupting the conversation.

The Marathas treated the Kathkaris in an obviously hostile way and we came across two cases of violence against the tribal community during our field trips. One case was of a man who wanted the panchayat to build a "pucca" house for him. He is reported to have mentioned to them his awareness about funds being used illegally. As a result he was stabbed by five Maratha men. Another was attacked because he had refused free liquor to Maratha customers. Both these cases typically reveal the attitude the Marathas in this village have towards the

Kathkaris, where they are probably continuing a policy of exploitation which they had with the dalits living in the same area some time ago.

Tara

The Marathas in a couple of other areas in the district, Tara village in Panvel Taluka, also reflected similar attitudes, but the situation in these cases did not seem to show this extent of exploitation. Tara mainly comprises an Agri settlement. Agris are a backward caste and are economically and politically dominant in this area. There are a few other settlements where both the Marathas and the Agris live; Barapada, a Muslim majority village which includes some Agris; Kathkariwadis, i.e. settlements of Kathkaris; and a number of private farms owned by businessmen from Bombay.

Pen

Pen Taluka, south of Panvel in which Tara falls, has villages of different or mixed communities, and a town which was once dominated by brahmins and kayasthas, but is now being increasingly inhabited by blue and white collar workers of the different industrial areas in Raigad. Here in the rural areas of the taluka, the Kathkaris live in separate settlements, away from the Maratha villages and the only interaction was during the seasons when Kathkari labour was required in the fields. Here again the Kathkaris were referred to as drunkards who never left the door till they were provided their daily ration of liquor, which had to accompany the daily wages. The tribal community was again condemned as a primitive and drunken society which would never get out of their situation.

But the Marathas and Kathkaris in these settlements did not acknowledge the existence of a major conflict or tension between the communities, perhaps because they lived in separate settlements, but more probably because both these areas have well entrenched voluntary organizations working with the tribals. The Yusuf Meherally Centre in Tara, has become an important landmark in the district known for its medical centre and the conducting of mass marriages for the Kathkaris. In Pen, the Development Research and Action Group is a major organization working with the Kathkaris and Thakurs.

Barsoli

One interesting encounter during our field visit to Barsoli, a settlement in Roha taluka, which has the largest concentration of industries in Raigad, was with a Maratha who had come to the Kathkari settlement to visit some members in a Kathkari family, who, he explained were his friends. He also pointed out that this family was economically in the same position as his own and that was why he considered them capable of being his friends, otherwise, in his own words, "who would befriend these drunken people?"

Agris

Tara

The Agris, a backward caste and a landed community in Tara village, also shared a similar perspective on the Kathkaris, who are employed by them as labourers on fields or brick-kiln sites. Once again the terms drunk and lazy were used, even as the older Agris of the village said that the Kathkaris were, at least earlier, more hardworking and less prone to drinking. This kind of sympathy was not shared by the younger Agris. They felt that it was no use helping the tribals because even as they got money it was spent immediately, because of a lack of incentive to save. At the same time they also acknowledged that the Kathkaris were a peaceful people who were very honest, and that they rarely found a Kathkari who was caught stealing. This is rather in contrast to earlier pre-independence descriptions of them as "criminal tribes".[1]

The younger Agris of this Tara village, a couple of whom owned brick-kilns, complained that the Kathkaris were not good labourers as far as brick-making was concerned and that was why they preferred getting Bhils and others from outside the district as far away as Jalgaon in Nashik district for the job. On inquiring we found that the Bhils demanded much less as wages, and it was this, rather than the Kathkari's supposed inability to do their job properly, that irritated these young men. One of them even went as far as to say that the Kathkaris should be dealt with very severely as they charged such high wages, and another was of the opinion that they should not be educated as this would result in a shortage of people willing to work as labourers, not an uncommon opinion among wage-labour employers.

Berle

On meeting members of the Agri community from Berle in Panvel taluka, we found the specific circumstances in that area giving rise to a different attitude towards the Kathkaris. Here they were anxious to present a picture of a peaceful relationship with the Kathkaris of the area. They said that they had good relations with the tribal community and most of them refrained from making disparaging remarks which was found in most of the other cases. We found that the Kathkaris in their neighborhood lived in a large settlement on the hillside, and they were an important source of labour for the Agris and also acted as a market for the goods sold by them in the Agri village.

At the same time these Kathkaris were members of the Ramdas movement, a local bhakti sect, which emphasized among other things, strict abstinence from alcohol and less strict vegetarianism. This movement had a serious following among the Kathkaris and also gave them a dignity which made its impact on the Agris in the plains nearby. These Agris were quite different, in comparison to other Agri communities, in their appraisal of the Kathkaris. The Agri teacher who worked in the primary school in the Kathkari settlement also had favourable things to say about the community. She said they were serious about giving up liquor and extremely cooperative when any work was required for the school.

We were, at the same time, aware that such statements could have been part of their official stance and that in private they may have had other things to say. But considering that members of other communities were open about their negative remarks, this official discourse was significant.

Thakurs

Meel

The Thakurs, or Thakkars, being scheduled tribes and more similar to the Kathkaris in terms of an economic and cultural lifestyle, had their own peculiarities in their perception of the Kathkaris. We met this community in Meel village near Khopoli, an industrialized town on the Bombay-Pune highway.

Some element of rivalry could be seen in the Thakurs' need to position themselves higher than the Kathkaris. Thus some of them claimed to use Brahmin priests during marriages, in which they also spent more money, while insisting that the Kathkaris did not do so. One woman did not hide her disgust at being compared to the Kathkaris, saying that her community was very different and did not eat monkeys and rats, which the Kathkaris did, and that their diet included only boars, chicken and goat. She also pointed out that they bury their dead while the Kathkaris cremate theirs. She also insisted that the Thakurs avoided eating and drinking in Kathkari houses while the latter could eat in theirs.

But during our discussions we were joined by a Kathkari man who was the forest watchman in the area and an obviously important person for the Thakurs. Many of them collected firewood from the forests to be sold in the markets down below and thus had to interact with him. We also discovered that his sister was the bhagat to whom a number of Kathkaris would go to when in need. In front of this man the discussion changed its course and they emphasized how good the relations between both the communities were. Yet there was a tendency to act as rivals, especially during the argument over which group spent more money during weddings!

Shedashi

Wherever there were Thakur settlements close to the Kathkari ones, there was a tendency of greater interaction as compared to other groups. In Shedashi Kathkariwadi in Pen taluka, we found that most males had disappeared into the Thakur neighbourhood for a video show. The Kathkaris are also regular customers if there are Thakur families selling liquor in the area.

In most of the cases the attitudes of the Thakurs towards the Kathkaris were shaped by a need to emphasize the differences between the communities in terms of beliefs, rituals and practices. Sometimes these differences would be stated in terms of a hierarchical relationship wherein both the communities claimed a superior status. At times they would be simply described as differences.

It must also be mentioned here that the Thakurs are often in a relatively better socio-economic position due to their success in liquor-making, a continuation of their traditional occupation of tapping toddy. This gives an air of credence to the Thakurs' claim of a higher status, which is then not contested by many Kathkaris who, as we shall see in the discussion later on, have internalized a poor self-image of themselves.

Social Workers

Stereotypes

The social workers who interact with the community also have their stereotypes, which may be reinforced or discarded according to the experience of the individual social worker. Different organizations may encourage their own peculiar perceptions of the community which influences their interactions with the Kathkaris in a particular way. The responses which we collected for this report were from the workers of the Janahit Vikas Trust, the NGO that participated in this study.

Most of the respondents saw the Kathkaris as victims of exploitation. Bonded labour, oppression from other groups and lack of land were seen as the main factors in this regard, and the lack of education was seen as the greatest obstacle to changing their situation. Addiction to liquor and a feeling of inferiority, were viewed as the Kathkaris' contribution to their present state of affairs.

On the other hand there were many qualities which were idealized. Their sense of belonging to the community was praised, evident in their serious participation in community meetings, at which they made it a point not to drink. The simple lifestyle and hospitality of the Kathkaris also came in for favorable comment, especially by the women social workers who pointedly emphasized how comfortable they were made to feel by the tribals, whenever they decided to stay the night over in their settlements. Even when drunk, they were reported to be very much in control of themselves, at least in the presence of the social workers.

Responses

But the workers also voiced their frustrations when working with the Kathkaris. Complaints of a slow and inconsistent response to the various activities of the organization and addiction to liquor, were listed as the main reasons for this. But these were not seen as unsurmountable obstacles and by and large the overall response was one of enthusiasm in working with the community. They felt it was not very difficult to chalk out the needs of specific settlements along with its members, who had a realistic understanding of their own situation. Most of the workers listed health, education, water and ownership of land as the main requirements of the Kathkaris.

At the same time many workers showed a concern for the increasing cases of wife-beating they came across, and the fact that women were often not allowed to speak at the meetings. This would indicate that they perceived the community's positive aspects without romanticizing them and yet were critical of what they considered to be the Kathkari's weak points. Such a perspective was by and large incorporated in their actual interaction especially, in their insistence that the members of the settlement play a responsible role in any of the programmes begun by the trust.

There were of course, exceptions at times among these social workers as well. Thus we also came across a number of terms such as "superstitious", "narrow-minded" and "lazy" used by some of them when referring to the Kathkaris. But by and large there was a certain caution in their speech, which must be heard in the context of the policies of the Janahit Vikas Trust itself. Undoubtedly these must have influenced the way the social workers perceived and related with the community. In this regard the trust has attempted to learn from the experiences of the Kune mission, and has made a conscious attempt to break away from past mistakes.

KATHKARI SELF-PERCEPTIONS

In their responses to our questioning the Kathkaris reveal a sharp and critical understanding of themselves and their position *vis-a-vis* other communities. It would be an obvious point to state that the Kathkari's perceptions of outside groups depend on their particular experiences with them, but it is important again, to keep this in mind as it would explain why we got such varying perceptions and attitudes.

Kathkaris as Adivasis

There was a near unanimous desire to discard the name Kathkari as a term of reference for themselves. In nearly all settlements, we came across this distaste for the word, and the explanation given was that it always elicited negative responses from other people. Youngsters complained that on their trips to other villages and towns when they were asked to identify themselves the term Kathkari got a mocking and çondescending response. In place of which they preferred the label 'adivasi' which they interpreted in their own way.

Significance of 'Adivasi'

There was a broad spectrum of meanings for this term which could be derived from their responses. It included principally those who are economically backward and the landless labourers. There were the more negative significations where the term seemed to imply illiterates, those who faced injustice and were seen as victims of exploitation. But a certain emphasis on the economic aspect of their identity could be discerned, thus the recurrent use of a term like *mazdoor*, labourer. Only once did we come across a reference to adivasis as being the lower most among all castes, but this was also interpreted by the Kathkari as implying the poorest group in the region.

Other communities were described as those having land, money and education. The dependence of the Kathkaris on them was pointed out frequently by the respondents, emphasizing an exchange where their subordination became the basis for defining their identity. Thus the interpretation of the term adivasis as labourers, those who have no land, those who work on the land of the Maratha/Agri, and so on.

Reactions to 'Kathkari'

At the same time the distaste of the term Kathkari revealed a motivation on their part to contest the perceptions which other groups had and which the Kathkaris felt were negative ones. Their self-perception thus revealed an acknowledgement of their subordinate economic position in the region and also a resistance to the negative perceptions which neighbouring groups had of them, which could add upto a quest for a new, more dignified identity.

It was only in Hemdi, a settlement in Pen taluka, that we did not come across an aversion to the name 'Kathkari'. Our inquiries revealed that this could be because of its own peculiar history. This settlement was a beneficiary of the Bhoodan movement in the years after independence and many members had received land. At the same time the Kune mission had also played an important role in the field of education and a number of children were sent to Nasik for schooling. We came across two men from the village who had been schooled by the mission and who were employed by the Tribal Welfare Department in the nearby town. The members of this settlement did not seem to impute a negative meaning too the term 'Kathkari', though they were aware that the term 'adivasi' was also used when referring to them.

One more example of their loyalty to their traditional identity could be seen in their responses to the overtures made by some Protestant groups which initially wanted them to replace pictures of their gods with those of Jesus. But the ensuing debate with the naik, where he argued against the possibility of changing his Kathkari identity as he was born into it, made them modify their stand and only asked the tribals to incorporate the image of Christ along with the other deities who already were present in their homes!

This was an exception to the other settlements which we came across, where they were only willing to give up their earlier label and opt for a term which they interpreted as being some kind of an economic category. This move of attempting to re-label their identity has many implications. On the one hand it reveals a realistic understanding of their position today, and also reveals a certain openness to change, while on the other it acknowledges a poor self-image as they accept the negative connotations of the term Kathkari. So even as they opt for a new label it does not necessarily imply the attainment of a better self-image, but at least it seems to indicate a felt need for one.

Inclusive Origins

Many respondents during our visits discussed the possible origins of the Kathkaris. One naik from Bhuneshwar gave us his version where the credit of creating the first Kathkari went to the god Ram, when he killed the monkey king Bali and asked the Kathkari whom he had just created, to eat up the corpse as no one else ate this species of animals. He went on to explain that the Kathkaris were very much like Ram as they also used bows and arrows like him. They also identified with the *Pandavas* from the *Mahabharata* for much the same reason.

This identification with the heroes from the epic, but in the idiom of their own culture, shows how the Kathkaris interpret symbols from mainstream Hinduism while also keeping a certain distance from it. This could be seen when the naik negated the cultural taboos of the outsiders, and disregarded upper-caste rules for food in explaining his version of Kathkari origins. Yet, this myth also acknowledged the importance of sanction from mainstream Hinduism, when its author claimed that this story was actually true and existed in the 'real' *Ramayana* which, he informed us was a 'thick' one and not easily available. This authority of the written word may have been a recent entry into their world but is symbolic of their subordination in a context where literacy is now such an important social requirement for any kind of socio-economic status.

Along with this interpretation of their origins the naik also gave us his theories on the history of the Kathkaris in more tangible terms. He claimed that the Kathkaris were of Bhil origin and had migrated from Gujarat. When asked where he had got this idea he said that he had travelled a lot, had met many people and had observed things. We wanted to know whether this notion was shared by other settlements but our inquiries found a number of contradictory responses. Some said that it was true but others denied it completely insisting that the Kathkaris and Bhils were very different. A few agreed that the community had come from Gujarat but insisted that they were never a part of the Bhils. At the same time these respondents said that the Bhils, Warlis and Kathkaris were all adivasis.

This seemed to us a significant point, as it indicated a move towards an inclusive identity giving them an affiliation with other communities with which they did not have any interaction whatsoever, but still perceived as having a common tradition. There were quite a few instances where we came across this affiliation with the Warlis and Bhils even as they emphasized that they were different groups.

We came across another settlement near Pui village where the members had quite a complex understanding of their history. Our first respondent here was very articulate, and his views were generally agreed to by other participants in the discussion. There seemed to be a general consensus on his story when we discussed it with other groups in the settlement. Later on, we came to know of the considerable influence of this man, who was a *bhagat,* among these people. He seemed very informed about the Kathkari community and acted as their representative in political matters.

Flexible Self-understanding

The story which emerged from our discussions attempted to give some sense of history to the community. The Kathkaris of the past were seen as "the kings of the jungle", a people of the forest. But there was no nostalgia or romanticism about the past. They saw themselves as people who "ate anything", and one respondent recited a well known Kathkari song which, when translated, means, "eaters of radish and carrots, kings of the jungle...." There seemed to be a sense of amusement when they described themselves in the past. "We lived like monkeys", was what one respondent told us. This tendency to laugh at their past may be interpreted as an example of a rather poor notion of self-worth, but it also signifies a willingness to come to terms with the present in a more realistic way, where they feel a need to adapt to new situations.

At the same time there is an awareness that the present is also not giving them a fair deal. Thus, as their story continues, they claim that outsiders came and cut down their forests, forcing them to change. They then had to live like "city-dwellers", but as they had no money or land they were just labourers, who had to live on the margins of the outside world.

This explanation reveals a conscious political understanding of the past, as an explanation of their present situation and a potential for change in a specific direction. As later on the discussion will reveal, the willingness of the Kathkaris to educate themselves in the formal sense of the term, can be seen as linked to this perception of their situation, where they see education as an important way of getting an adequate livelihood, which is not dependent on wage labour. At the same time an equally important premium is given to land as they realize that it is the only resource which can substitute the forests in providing them a livelihood in place of their present dependence on the labour market.

Both these needs are implied in their self-perception. Their identity is directly linked to their political present, even as it is flexible enough to allow them their choices for the future. The constant reference to other communities which they encounter, thus becomes an organic factor in understanding themselves.

Attitudes to Others

While most respondents stated that their relationship with Agris or Marathas was one where the Kathkaris were dependent on them for their livelihood, very rarely did we get any indication of reverence or an acknowledgement of their superiority in terms of ritual or cultural practices. Their dependence was seen because they did not have land, money or education while the Agris or Marathas had all three, thus making such a relationship of dependency possible. If ever there was mention of any injustices faced by the community it was attributed to the fact that they lacked economic power and it was added that this was a situation which could change once their economic position improved.

Berle

In Berle, a settlement in Panvel taluka, we found a very critical attitude towards the Agri village down below. It was stated that even though presently their relation with the Agris was fairly amicable, it was very different some years ago. Even quite recently, the naik informed us, some Agris did not allow them to use the well during the summer and that they looked down upon the Kathkaris.

However, he claimed that things were now definitely better than before. Then the Agris did not respect the Kathkaris at all, and treated them in a condescending manner. Things only changed when there was a physical fight between the communities, following the beating of an old Kathkari by some Agris, as he had no money to pay for his liquor from an Agri shop. The Kathkaris then attacked and claimed to have defeated the Agris in a combat. This incident was viewed by them as being instrumental in increasing the dignity of the Kathkaris, as they claimed that following it the Agris began looking on them with new respect, for now a Kathkari could walk through the village in a proud and fearless manner.

This story reveals the desire of the Kathkaris to be viewed with, what can only be referred to as, dignity, and also shows that more often than not, they do not actually experience it. In this particular case the Kathkaris actually managed to create a myth over an incident which made it possible to change certain perceptions, and demand, at least in the public sphere, a respect which they felt was theirs. Of course this village was one where the Kathkaris were particularly large in number and were influenced strongly by the Ramdas bhakta movement. Both these factors played their roles in giving them a strong feeling of pride and perhaps a greater sensitivity to the question of 'dignity'.

It would also not be too out of place to mention that in this settlement the men openly looked down upon jobs like fishing and collecting firewood, a task thus forced upon women, and that many young men could be found idling away their time in the afternoons, as the work that they preferred doing was something in the towns and cities, which few could actually get.

On being asked whether they considered the Agris in any way superior, they disagreed, adding at the same time that they did treat those Agris with respect, who happened to employ them. Such a response was quite frequent, where they acknowledged the superior position of the landed communities and their condescending attitude towards the Kathkaris, at the same time revealing their resentment at this attitude claiming that it was tolerated only because they were in a weak position and that it would change once their situation improved. One came across resentments against Agris who would have meetings to decide the wage rates of the Kathkari labourers without consulting the Kathkaris themselves; yet there was a helplessness, as they found that little could be done about it.

Later we will focus on this perception of their life where power is strongly linked to economic assets and not much attention seems to be paid to formal political processes which may actually be related to their situation.

Shedashi

An interesting case was of a landowning Kathkari who responded to our query, by mockingly telling us that he considered the Marathas inferior to him as it was they who worked on his fields as labourers. This particular man had even managed to give loans to members of other communities who mortgaged their land in return.

In Shedashi we came across some Kathkaris telling us that the Thakurs were inferior to them as they too sold their labour and were dependent on the Kathkaris as the latter bought liquor from them. But this view was contested by the Thakurs, whom we met later, who felt just the opposite. And even as these Kathkaris claimed their superiority others in the same group contradicted them by saying that the Thakurs had grown rich because they manufactured liquor, but were not drunkards, while the Kathkaris themselves were so addicted to alcohol that they wasted all their money on this habit.

What we observed in this village was a sustained interaction between the two communities. The Thakurs having electricity in their village often managed to organize video shows of Hindi and Marathi films for which the Kathkaris were always a ready audience. Even during festivals both the communities would celebrate them together.

Killa

In Killa, where their relationship with the Marathas was problematic, the Kathkaris were quite critical of this dominant group but at the same time acknowledged their superiority. They knew that their entire settlement was completely dependent on the Marathas, as all government welfare schemes had to come via the village panchayat. They informed us that the Marathas had siphoned off large amounts of money, especially in the housing schemes and that they were deliberately creating disunity and suspicion among the Kathkaris. Their view of the Marathas was one where the dominant group was seen as an exploitative one, yet when we saw the Marathas openly insulting the Kathkaris by abusing them, they would keep quiet.

It was later explained that there was no use fighting because then the Marathas would harass them in other ways. But with the start of the Konkan railway work in that area, the Kathkaris have an alternative to working for the Marathas. It was significant that the Marathas complained to us about the Kathkaris running away to the railway sites for work even as the railways did not give them food, tea and liquor, besides the daily wages, as the Marathas did, and this was presented as one more evidence of their "ungratefulness".

In this settlement we saw a more obvious exploitation of the tribal community which made them see the dominant group in a particular way, and which shaped their understanding of their own identity. In this case it was an acknowledgement of their dependence and their helplessness in changing the situation.

Ambiguities and Self-depreciation

Thus the Kathkaris specific experiences with other communities influenced their perception of themselves. When they claimed that other groups were superior, inferior or at the same level, and our experiences showed a range of responses based on all these statements, they were attempting to place themselves in the wider cultural and political scheme of things and thus defining their identity in a particular way.

As discussed earlier our interaction with the community revealed a very critical outlook, where their economic needs were seen as organically linked to that of dignity. So while the dominant groups were viewed as such, simply because they had the resources, it was also mentioned that they themselves would come up to that position once they too got control of such assets, whether it was land, employment or education.

Such an understanding at once resented any condescending and mocking attitude by the dominant groups and this was why they laid such a premium on using a different term of reference for themselves. At the same time they often showed a self-critical outlook, when they blamed their drinking as a major obstacle to their advancement.

But in spite of observing such a complex understanding amongst the community, it was difficult to ignore a certain self-depreciation which accompanied their discussions. The very act of accepting the negative associations with the term Kathkari, leading to the desire for a change of name, shows the success of the dominant groups in influencing the Kathkaris in a way that suits their interests. The consequent distancing which the Kathkaris then desire from the label also signifies a distancing from their own past and earlier way of life which becomes associated with symbols which are seen as primitive and to be ashamed of.

Thus the dual consequence of this desire for change. The Kathkaris begin seeing their own way of life, especially as it was in the past, as one that is shameful and undesirable, and this at once undermining all their critical outlook emphasized earlier. So even as they may view their position in a realistic manner, they still live without dignity, as in their everyday interactions the dominant groups would keep reinforcing their self-image in a negative light, forcing them to be burdened with an undesirable vision of their past. In the next section of this analysis we discuss the second aspect of our inquiry, 'dignity'.

MARGINALIZATION AND MOBILITY

Change and mobility for the marginalized has often involved imitating more powerful and privileged groups and accepting their customs as superior. But this has not been a simple one-way process.

The interaction of such groups has also been underlined by exploitation and power games and even if the weaker groups take on the cultural traits of the dominant ones it does not mean acknowledging the superiority of the latter as much as that of an open rivalry and competition over resources between the concerned groups.

This is clearly seen with the Kathkaris. They do see the Marathas and Agris as the dominant ethnic groups in the area and even imitate their lifestyles. But this is not necessarily seen as a dilution of their own identity. On the contrary it is a means of strengthening their position in the vicinity and sharing the resources of the region. They become better Kathkaris as they get land, money and education.

Intergenerational Changes

The aspirations for the future which the Kathkaris have, can be perceived in the statements of the younger generation. Many young men we met, looked very different from their parental generation. Their hair cuts were indicative of their interaction with an urban milieu, as they were typical of the current fashion in the area. Their clothes often included shirts and *pants*, while the women continued with the *sari* but wore it like their Agri or Maratha neighbours. This is truer of those settlements which are closer to towns. In the interior villages a very small number may have changed their dress very noticeably, but the direction of their change is unmistakable.

Berle Youth

One group of Kathkari youth we came across at Berle were quite open in their criticism of their elders. They felt that as they had seen more of the world, their choices and demands were more realistic. A job with a government or a private firm was an urgent demand, and it was taken for granted that it was the man of the house who would take the job. While the women in the same village were busy on the fields the youth could be seen loitering around and openly looking with disdain at any work linked to physical labour or even agriculture.

The naik of this particular village felt that the young boys must be given a preference over girls in getting educated as they would be the ones who would get jobs outside. There was a definite tendency to push women away from the new competitive world, and relegate them more rigidly to household work. In their visits to towns and cities they see that the whole language of 'progress' has very little space for women's participation in the public sphere and thus, when they chalk out their own plans women are usually left out.

Now as the Kathkari himself is marginalized with his lack of skill in an industrialized world the situation becomes even more problematic, as he looks down upon his own traditional way of life and cannot be absorbed into a new one. While such a state of affairs may not be so obvious seen in the more isolated settlements, yet it is bound to affect them sooner or later.

In spite of such problems Berle Kathkariwadi is viewed as a model for the others in the vicinity. The members proudly claim that they have given up liquor, a habit which they themselves associate with their backwardness, no doubt reinforced by the superior attitude of the more privileged groups, but which is a real problem for the tribals.

Swami Ramdas Bhaktas

Much of the credit for the change among the Kathkaris of Berle goes to their long standing participation in the Swami Ramdas Bhakta movement referred to earlier. This is a religious movement which encourages vegetarianism, which is not strictly imposed, as well as abstaining from liquor, which is. Members go regularly to the weekly religious meetings in Kolke, a nearby village where other communities also come to listen to the local leader of the movement.

Those Kathkaris in the movement, whom we met in Berle had given up liquor. They showed a certain confidence and saw themselves as better off than other members of their own community. They now regularly bargain collectively for higher daily wages. No doubt this was made possible through a certain pride in themselves, for which one cannot underestimate the importance of the Ramdas movement.

The above analysis reveals the multifaceted complexity of their situation. On one hand there is the story of their success where they have managed to keep a standard of living much higher than many others in their own community even though a very small proportion of the entire wadi owns land. The sense of dignity and pride they have owes a lot to their religious motivation. Yet their real wants are not satisfied as their literacy level is low, and employment would thus be difficult in the formal economic sector. They feel that agriculture does not hold a future for them at all and the industrialized world is still not ready to absorb them. Moreover, in the direction they are moving women are being more and more marginalized in public social spaces.

Felt Needs and Anomalies

Basic Needs

Land, wages and education are among the most urgent demands listed by nearly all the settlements as being the most important requirements for the tribe. They are also the most popular issues for getting the Kathkaris to join rallies and demonstrations organized by voluntary agencies. Land and related assets like bullocks and implements for cultivation are listed as immediate demands by those settlements not yet touched by urbanization, while those closer to towns or industrialized centres talk in terms of regular jobs which provide monthly incomes.

Daily wages as well as work which involves physical labour are seen as demeaning which must be done away with as soon as possible. For their children they see education as the chief means through which this can be made possible.

Yet these are visions for the future. Their immediate needs more often than not include things as basic as water and housing. The summer months are long thirsty stretches for most Kathkaris, and even where taps or wells exist they run dry. The lack of water for drinking as well as cultivation is a major problem and underscores many other issues. It is also inevitably linked to health problems, which are all too inadequately tackled.

The housing schemes introduced by the state government and occasionally by the central government, are more often than not opportunities for local officials to make money. This was told to us in nearly all the settlements. In most cases the gram panchayats are in charge and manage to siphon off funds away from the intended purpose. Most houses we saw were made of substandard material and quite unlivable during the monsoons. So this also was listed as an immediate demand.

Both, water and housing, show the amount of dependence of the Kathkaris on external agents for such basic needs. They realize that their habitats have changed beyond recognition and their own efforts to adapt seem inadequate. The details of the corruption responsible for swindling them of their land and other resources are well known to all of them, and were told to us in unambiguous terms during our discussions.

In Killa, where the Kathkaris were directly controlled by the gram panchayat dominated by the Marathas of the village, we were told of stories of violence perpetuated on the adivasis by the dominant caste. The dependence on the Marathas for their daily income and also aspects like housing and water created a situation where naked exploitation was rampant. Even as we interviewed the people, some Maratha men would follow and interrupt the discussions. This gave us an idea of the kind of change expected from the Kathkaris and the odds faced by them in trying to achieve it.

Forest Access

A large proportion of their income also comes from selling firewood and here they have to combat local forest officials who often take away their sickles or fine them when they are caught collecting wood. More often than not they are bribed by the tribals. We came across one Kathkari forest watchman who lived with the Dhangars, a shepherd community, near a forest in Khopoli taluka. He referred to the trees as his children. He said that his higher-ups would bring along businessmen to cut a large number of trees, while he himself was ticked off if he allowed local Thakurs to collect firewood. The members of the wadi informed us that even this watchman was not averse to taking an occasional bribe. But the level of exploitation at which he operates and that of his seniors are completely different in kind not just degree.

The forests by now have entirely lost their earlier relevance to the adivasis. Some youth who were going off to sell firewood, informed us that they cut wood indiscriminately and did not think it their concern to plant more trees. The reason they gave for doing this was that anyway they would not be allowed to use the firewood and thus felt no obligation to grow trees. Earlier they were particular about which trees to avoid cutting as some were considered sacred, but now they do not bother, as long as nobody ever comes to know. All this refers to a tremendous change in their world view, a legacy of the commercial exploitation of forests initiated on a large scale by the British government and carried on more ruthlessly even today.

Voluntary Agencies

Yet in recent years afforestation schemes have proved to be very popular with the Kathkaris as the soil is good for growing fruit trees which have a high commercial value. Many voluntary agencies are involved with this scheme and we came across a number of settlements where afforestation programmes had begun.

As mentioned earlier liquor consumption is a major problem listed by the Kathkaris themselves as an obstacle to their adaption to a changing environment. Berle Kathkariwadi is a striking exception mainly due to the long standing influence of the Ramdas bhakta movement discussed earlier. Certainly tribal alcoholism has not at all helped them in making what they themselves would feel are the right social and economic choices. In the other settlements while drinking is a must during festivals and celebrations, it is strictly avoided during meetings where serious discussions are held.

Poultry cooperatives and keeping of goats were other schemes which they felt would be of immediate benefit to them. In Koralwadi, a poultry cooperative was begun and subsequently stopped, because the hens were of a breed which could not survive without special food. Though, for a brief time that they lived their eggs brought in good money. But they soon died and the others could not be sold in the market as they were not to the local taste. The members told us that the scheme should be revived but with country hens, more resilient to local conditions. This was agreed to even by other settlements. Goats were also productive economically, both for milk as well as for their capacity to provide manure in the fields. Thus aid from various agencies in this regard was perceived by them as being very helpful.

We found in their responses a very realistic understanding of their economic and political choices, with regard to both long-term and short-term gains. The detailed discussions regarding their needs as well as the obstacles faced by them in this regard showed an active mind, which has managed to grasp the complexity of their situation quite well. Though in some cases the stories of the social workers regarding their difficulty in getting the adivasis to actually cooperate with them in implementing their schemes may have some truth to them, there are an equal number of cases where they have shown a remarkable initiative in doing things without any outside help, especially when they have had the security of individual land ownership or the advantage of a responsible leadership.

Conscientization and Education

Electoral Politics

The Kathkaris show little interest in electoral politics. In most cases we came across a certain disillusionment with such political processes. In a couple of settlements we were told that they voted alternatively for the Congress-I, the Shetkari-Kamgar Paksha and the Peasants and Workers Party, with equal detachment and no hope of any useful returns. Most political parties competing with each other seemed to show little interest in them probably because they often left their homes for other places in the district looking for jobs.

In some cases, though the Congress-I state government had introduced a number of schemes, their actual implementation through local structures more often than not did not really reach the intended people. This was discussed above in the case of building pucca houses. In one case the adivasis were forced to vote for a party against their wishes because of threats of physical violence from the dominant caste of the village. This is hardly surprising, where governmental structures at the local level usually consist of the dominant castes which do not feel any urge to respond to the legitimate needs of the subordinate groups.

Responsible Leadership

The Kathkaris are also aware that a responsible leadership can be an important agent of change. The very fact that they disregard the hereditary line if they find the naik not responsible shows the importance attached to the leader. In spite of the negative self-perception they sometimes reveal they also see hard work and honesty in themselves, which gives them a sense of pride. These sentiments can be helpful in moving the community in the direction of self-reliance and independence.

The voluntary agencies working with them have been an important catalytic presence for their conscientization. From fighting for land rights to organizing income-generation schemes, these organizations have had a major impact on their lives. Some settlements had members who were very active in the Kathkari Mukti Sanghatana, a movement for re-acquiring possession of their land.

The contrast between those Kathkari settlements which are close to industrial centres is striking and summarizes in a compelling image the situation of the Kathkaris in this fast changing geographic area. For here we see juxtaposed two economies, two modes of resource use that are centuries apart technologically.

Education and Employment

In today's contexts the Kathkaris make a connection between formal education and employment and see it as an important agent of change. They feel that without it adjusting to the new environment was difficult, if not impossible.

In Koralwadi, near Tara village, we came across an individual who was given a permanent job in a factory of a large company, but who found the pressures of a fixed time-bound framework a difficult thing to get adjusted to. He was found sleeping on the job a number of times or absenting himself because he had gone to collect firewood. After a number of warning letters he finally took his provident fund and left. Many of them see this as a failure to adapt, and want formal education for their children to avoid such situations.

It was undeniable that education was given a high priority by most settlements and they saw in it a possibility for their children to escape from the lifestyle in which they were trapped revolving around physical labour, daily wages and indebtedness.

But in cases where the children who had managed to study up till their high school and still did not get the kind of work they hoped for, the disillusionment was stronger. Formal education raises expectations for a better job and a higher status and if agencies want their educational programmes to be a success they must ensure some kind of a linkage with economic betterment. The difficulty actually is that no agency by itself can claim to be a real help to the adivasis. What is needed is a multipronged approach to the complex changes this kind of a society is undergoing. While education is an important agent in this process it is not enough by itself to guarantee a secure future.

CONCLUSIONS

Our participatory fieldwork gives us a clearer idea of the situation of the Kathkaris, even though it convinces us that there are no easy answers to their problems. They are a people quite aware of the complexity of their world but this very quality makes it difficult to talk in terms of quick solutions. At the same time this does not indicate a move towards complacency but should actually encourage these tribals, and those working with them, to tackle their problems with a more critical eye. To this end we shall now try to bring together some of the more pertinent findings before they can be discussed in greater depth with regard to their wider significance in the next chapter.

Emerging Orientations

The fact that the tribal community is discarding its old name, 'Kathkari', for a more inclusive and, according to their interpretation, a predominantly economic category, i.e. 'adivasi', reveals an interesting critical response to their present situation. In giving up the old label they are expressing a need to break away from the past and along with it, memories of being subservient labourers. As 'adivasis' they are now identifying with the economically underprivileged, the oppressed, who are forced to survive by their physical labour, as *'Kashtakaris'* or the toiling masses.

Hence land issues are an important point around which a large number of Kathkaris come together for morchas and demonstrations. Various voluntary organizations have played helpful roles in mobilizing and motivating them. The more established settlements have been conscientized to demand electricity, water supply and brick-built, pucca, houses.

But the continuing ecological degradation in the district accentuates their poverty, as basic needs, like food, shelter and clothing, become scarce. In a region with a generous monsoon and numerous streams, the polluted rivers and water scarcity in the district, especially acute in the summers, are the most visible signs of such degradation.

Gender inequality too has been affected by the socio-economic changes the Kathkaris are undergoing. Traditionally tribal society has been more egalitarian than caste communities, especially on the gender dimension. In fact gender inequality increased with upper-caste status. Now with greater competition for employment in the job market, and upper-caste role models, women are being more and more restricted to the unorganized sector and household chores. The unfortunate rise in wife-beating remarked by the social workers, only underlines tribal women's declining status.

However, a positive development among these Kathkaris is their changed attitude to education. The response to the adult education programmes in the area would indicate that they realize that education for employment may now be a missed opportunity for the older generation, but they do not want the same to happen to their children. This is a qualitatively different situation from the difficulties the Kune mission met in trying to entice these 'children of the forest' to school.

Their willingness to have their children educated is another important indicator of their desire to be integrated into the mainstream of the society around them. Though here boys are given preference over girls in education as later too in the job market.

Yet the desire to see their children in the government and the administrative sector or in the nearby industries is very clearly a desire to be involved with the rapidly changing world around them, and escape from the torment of forced physical labour. Unfortunately even now, very few of them eventually are absorbed by the modern sector of the economy and most have no choice but to continue being unskilled labourers, ever more inhumanly exploited and oppressed.

Education and Tribal Mobility

One effective way of empowering the marginalized to challenge this monopoly of power, is through conscientization and education. Given the new found openness among the tribals to both these a positive beginning has been definitively made. For formal education is clearly something they now want for their children, though this is a long term, almost a generational investment in eventual structural change.

On the other hand, non-formal education centres, women's groups, adult literacy classes may not give the impression of deep structural changes operating in the area, especially as the agencies involved often look for quick results and the people, in turn, for even quicker economic pay offs. But if one observes the strong dominant caste influence on the psyche of the tribals, which these agencies themselves concede is very detrimental to a positive self-image for them then one must see these programmes as something more than what their immediate effects might indicate.

For they create spaces which allow for the kind of interaction which makes for more positive notions of self-worth. If such non-formal education is combined with effective income generation schemes, only then can such marginalized groups exercise a greater measure of control over their own lives.

But here again, while formal education better prepares the individual tribal for the changes and challenges of today than their own traditional processes of socialization would, it almost inevitably also estranges the educated tribals from their own community. This results in individual advancement at best, but little or no upward social mobility for the community at large. For education to become a movement among the Kathkaris a more imaginative and flexible system, tuned to their special needs, is required. The present *ashramshalas* are a long way off from this ideal, and are moving very hesitantly, if at all, in this direction.

Yet the logic of an industrializing region demands an importance given to formal education and the upgradation of skills, even though education can reinforce hierarchies to the disadvantage of the less educationally qualified. However, this only further underscores the importance of neutralizing this disadvantage with some kind of protective discrimination for these marginalized tribals. It would be most unfair to allow them to be deprived of the opportunities that the education system does open up, as in fact is now happening.

But the intervening agencies must also include a critical perspective in their educational programmes. They must make educational institutions more responsive to the needs of the community, and encourage a more critical outlook, so that when really helpful alternatives are possible the community makes the right social choices.

At present the formal system only distances the tribals from their community, while assimilating them into the larger society around. How this is to be remedied is a complex issue beyond the scope of this study, yet no less an urgent task all the same.

Continuity and Change

In presenting a reconstruction of their past with the perceptions of their present, the change from pre- to post- colonial forms of social organization should not be exaggerated. Rather what stands out is the continuing group identity throughout their changing circumstances. For our analysis reveals that even as the Kathkaris had responded in the past, to different changes in the economic and political structure of the region, this did not mean any final drastic dissolution of their identity as a distinctive group. They adapted to specific circumstances in their history, forging different kinds of relationships with other neighbouring groups.

The pre-colonial forms of economic and political organization in the region encouraged the production, consumption and exchange of commodities based on small community units. As Ernest Gellner points out.[2] Hence each community had its own particular niche within the system, though those in closer and more constant interaction inevitably came to be more absorbed and integrated into the caste hierarchy. But this did not add up to a dissolution of their ethnic identities, even though there was a tendency to imitate the more dominant upper-caste groups, as for instance with sanskritization or ksyatriyization. More often than not such a process of adaptation implied a conflict over resource use as different groups competed with each other to advance their own group status.

However, this cannot be mistaken for a movement towards homogenization. For group identities were being strengthened through this process as the dominant economic and political structures were still dependent on a technology for production that was rooted in community organization. A group like the Kathkaris may not have been deeply entrenched in the caste hierarchy, as the forests provided an alternative to a complete dependence on caste society. But as this becomes less and less viable, they become correspondingly more and more dependent on wage labour for the landed dominant castes.

The accompanying adoption of upper-caste customs and mores, mentioned by various historical sources, is really an attempt on their part to strengthen their own position in the larger society with which they are come into contact. The heterogeneity within the Kathkari community itself, only goes to show their uneven relationships with other groups in this process of acculturation. Those groups that did not accept certain upper-caste taboos were the less dependent ones. But as the pattern of resource use in the region changed, so too did the different group dependencies.

The story of colonialism and its impact on such relations has been illustrated with the example of the Kathkaris responses to colonial expansion in western India. Modern economic systems have thrived on homogenized markets and centralized production, even as interest groups operate to dominate and control resources. Traditionally powerful groups continue to dominate economic organization even in the modern context.

For the tribals this centralization implied an increased dependency as alternative modes of survival, like the forests in this instance, were exhausted or appropriated by dominant groups. Physical and menial labour now becomes the only alternative and is exploited by the dominant groups in the economy which are in a position to dictate the terms of employment. This is exactly where we find the Kathkaris today.

Even as social change is very visible at the level of a changing lifestyles, traditionally dominant groups continue to exploit resources to their own advantage. Thus a system which centralizes technology allows for such groups to gain greater control, with the consequent greater dependence of weaker groups on them. So also does the centralization of markets over a wider area also allow some more dominant groups to further increase their monopoly control.

Already nativistic ideologies of preference for 'sons of the soil' are being propagated by chauvinistic political parties in this region. The Shiv Sena already has a base with youth groups and trade unions, and is promising to ensure that jobs in the local industries go to local youth. Of course the underprivileged groups, like the Thakurs, Kathkaris, etc., are not be given the same consideration as the upper-caste groups, especially as party organizations are dominated by the latter. Yet underprivileged groups do join such movements, and are all too often coopted by vested interests.

Ethnic Identity and Marginalization

The Kathkari profile that finally emerges from these last two chapters demonstrates a not unexpected correspondence between perceptions of tribal identity and evaluations of their human dignity. A negative perception of tribal cultural identity goes with a devaluation of their human worth, whether this be in the perceptions of others or in their own self-perceptions. In other words, a loss of ethnic identity corresponds to a marginalization in their social status, and vice versa.

For what is more noteworthy is that these perceptions are themselves closely related to the exchange relations prevalent between these tribals and the outsiders. The traditional terms of exchange are being rapidly replaced by increasingly unfavourable ones, over which they have no control, and from which there is no escape. And so their progressive marginalization seems inevitable.

Yet there are a few instances where an individual or a group have been able to stay or reverse this trend for themselves. For example: a Kathkari owning land employing non-Kathkaris on it; or a Kathkaripada bargaining collectively for better wages. Such affirmations do make for more positive perceptions of the Kathkaris, and even though resented by the non-Kathkaris affected, they still help gain their respect, however grudgingly.

Obviously though, these are more the exceptions than the rule, and if this trend is to develop into a movement, something more decisive by way of facilitation will be necessary on a larger scale to precipitate the structural change needed, in order to re-establish more equitable exchange relations for these tribals. But this will require a rather different approach from the present paternalistic welfare and top-down development plans being promoted.

For the confidence which such groups require can be greatly helped by some form sustained interaction with people and agencies without any other vested interest to compromise them, who deal respectfully with the tribals on an everyday basis. Such agencies can become effective reference groups for the tribals, if indeed they live close enough to them, and thus displace the dominant influence of upper-caste groups, subtly but effectively.

While stressing the importance of the material basis of these exchange relations we are not opting for a reductionist political economy approach. For exchange relations are not just imposed from without by an unequal power equation. There are, besides, characteristics that have become intrinsic to a group, that permit, and at times could even promote, an iniquitous relationship, at the group's own cost. Thus for the tribals the prevalence of alcoholism makes them extremely vulnerable to such outside impositions and exploitation, since it saps their resilience and their will to resist from within, trapping them ever more unrelentingly in their poverty.

The Ramdas Bhakta movement in this area has over the years successfully countered this threat, though it has done so by drawing the tribals closer into the Hindu fold. Yet, even as this movement is changing the identity of its Kathkari following, it is helping them to enhance their collective self-image, and thus provide an effective basis for resisting exploitation rather than submitting to it helplessly.

The links which have been forged between liquor and wage labour in this region is an important factor in perpetuating tribal poverty. But attempts at discouraging liquor drinking remains problematic, without some deeper motivation and even a mass movement as the recent one against arrack in Andhra. In this connection, the success of the Swamiramdas bhakta movement has surely something to do with the cultural space it affords the Kathkaris to interact with and feel accepted by the better off castes and classes.

But as urbanization begins to encroach on such spaces, they may once again find themselves no better off than before. Indeed there is little reason to feel that in such circumstances they would be any the less vulnerable, than similarly placed poor people in our cities, to the anomie and alienation that is their unenviable and unrelenting lot.

For in the competition between groups in the district for their place in the sun, the more dominant ones like the Marathas and Agris manage to secure jobs provided by the vast infrastructure, though of course, the most privileged at the top are mostly from outside the district. The competition within various groups benefits the relatively better off and marginalize the disadvantaged groups, like the Kathkaris, who are marginalized further at the bottom.

However, if the lost and the lonely, the poorest and the least among us are to be freed from the vicious circle of deprivation, and not left marginalized in our society, what is needed is a reorientation of our developmental priorities. For the present ones have precipitated a consumerism that seems to be both the vehicle and the goal of our developmental process. In actuality, this has only hastened environmental degradation and accentuated social inequalities, and now seems to be gaining a further boost in its momentum with the new economic policy.

But too often does a critique of high consumption lifestyles, romanticize traditional tribal culture, instead of reorienting our planning priorities and placing the tribals themselves, and other such marginalized groups at the centre of our developmental concerns. In other words, putting Gandhi's last Indian first.

REFERENCES

1. Cf. Kennedy, cited in Zimmermann, *op. cit.*, p. 8.
2. Ernest Gellner, *Culture, Identity and Politics*, Cambridge University Press, Cambridge, 1987, pp.13-17.

5

TRIBAL IDENTITY AND DIGNITY
An Integrative Response

RECAPITULATION

In attempting a definition of a 'tribe' in the first chapter we ended up with a 'descriptive' 'ethnic category', a 'colonial administrative construct', a 'contemporary ideological concept'. These add up at the most to an operational delineation of the term. In our historical perspective a tribe was better identified as a stage in the evolutionary process, and because of their particular histories, tribal groups find themselves at different stages and changing at varied paces in this process. Hence, we must be sensitive to inter-tribal diversity and recognize "that there is not one tribal system but many, that there is not one but several tribal economies".[1] In fact we need to be aware of intra-tribal differentiation as well. Indeed, "except for a few isolated and small communities, no tribe in India today subsists on a single techno-economy of production".[2]

No wonder then from the earliest studies by colonial administrators and other pioneers to

> the bulk of contemporary writings on adivasis, the term 'tribe' has remained vague, not adequately conceptualized and, consequently, of weak methodological value.... Most Indian 'tribal studies' have remained synchronic and descriptive, ignoring the economic and political transformations that affected the populations studied.[3]

Now if the 'fundamental issues' on the tribal question that were raised at the end of the first chapter are to be faced, issues of equity, sustainability, participation, autonomy, integration, then, we must go beyond such 'vague' and 'weak' descriptive studies of our "indigenous ethnic minorities, to a more profound analysis of the mechanisms perpetuating their subjugation and subordination".[4]

For the Kathkaris we began this task in chapter three by reconstructing an historical profile, and in chapter four, contextualizing this in contemporary perceptions. Overall, what emerges from this analysis is that to reverse the unequal exchange that has marginalized these tribals, the material basis for this must be changed, and only some form of positive discrimination in their favour will be able to achieve this. Moreover, to make this tribal development into an effectively self-sustaining process, a positive self-image and group identity is necessary, and this is not helped by paternalistic welfarism.

Most tribal protest movements have successfully mobilized such identities, and if the Kathkaris are too small a tribal to precipitate a revolution in their area, it is certainly feasible to facilitate a process of developmental change for them by doing likewise. This brings us to the issue of ethnicity as a response to the tribal question that we began with.

Here we argue that to preserve the identity and dignity of these threatened people today, tribal ethnicity needs to be mobilized to overcome their minority status, so that in their integration into the national mainstream, the distinctive contribution they make will be appreciatively accepted, and the incisive challenge they pose honestly faced by this larger society.

APPROACHES TO ETHNICITY

In the seventies

> a vast range of phenomena formerly subsumed under tribal, cultural, linguistic and religious differences, became increasingly identified with the term ethnicity despite some initial resistance.[5]

But theoretical perspectives were slower to change. Thus in the Indian situation Surajit Sinha already in 1965 spoke of 'tribes' as 'certain ethnic groups',[6] and S. C. Dube introduces 'tribal ethnicity' in 1977.[7] More recently others have used the term more analytically. Here we will first try to clarify the discourse before proceeding with our analysis.

Concept and Context

In trying to reach the substantive core of 'ethnicity' and to set it in our tribal context we must at the outset realize that "there never has been a single discourse of ethnicity. Rather there have been a plurality of discourses."[8] Our purpose, however, is not to deal with just "the theoretical construct created by social theorists to catalogue phenomena and social groups," but rather to "encounter ethnicity as actually lived, as a dynamic process with a specific present, entailing a particular mode of social experience".[9] Ethnicity, then, is here treated as a dynamic historical phenomenon, not a static conceptual category.

Hence we will not enter some of the overly theoretical debates: between the 'primodialists', for whom the ethnic group is based on a natural, primordial bond, and the 'instrumentalists' who stress its utilitarian and rational basis; or the 'survivalists', who see ethnic forms changing but not disappearing, and the 'evolutionists', who hold that these will eventually yield to a more democratic, socialist participation; or the 'maximalists', who limit ethnicity to strong and violent manifestations and the 'minimalists', who include weak and symbolic expressions as well.[10]

Broadly speaking ethnicity refers to a collective identity based on some common characteristics. Lists of these characteristics have been made to arrive at some kind of common substantive core. But as with the concept of 'tribe', here too there is much overlap and even arbitrariness apparent in these listings. Obviously, any collective identity will have some content to it. But what this content will be, and how the group comes to an awareness of it, will depend on who is defining this identity and how it articulates with others in that society. For besides the objective basis, as, if not more important for ethnic identities, is the subjective construct. It is this which can create and legitimize such ethnic groups as in the case of "imagined communities",[11] and "the invention of traditions".[12] Moreover, "as collective identities practiced in everyday life",[13] these ethnic identities must change as the group evolves.

Thus, while the objective features constitute a basis for an ethnic group the boundary is delimited by the group's changing subjective consciousness. Hence for our purposes here, an

> ethnic group is a historical entity whose members in large part conceive of themselves as being alike by virtue of certain common stable features located in language, culture, stereotypes, territory, ancestry--real or fictitious, specific nomenclature and endogamy and are so regarded by the members of other ethnic groups.[14]

Now while none of these features are by themselves indispensable, the operative ones add up to what has been variously called "primordial sentiments",[15] "core values",[16] "symbolic estates",[17] "corporate holdings".[18] Now, however basic or 'primordial' these core features may be, in so far as they are part of a 'constructed identity', they are never immutable or static, but always responsive to the eco-political and socio-cultural context in a concrete historical situation.

It is only when ethnicity is conceptualized in such a relational context that it can be a useful analytical tool. But unfortunately not all approaches to ethnicity have been sensitive to this.

Perspectives on Ethnicity

The earliest attempts at constructing ethnic identities for the tribal world were usually by outsiders imposing ethnocentric stereotypes that were largely negative and/or patronizing, as for instance, the 'noble savage' or 'the inscrutable Indian'. This reflected more the West's need to come to terms with the 'other', the non-western world, more than the historical reality and experience of these people. In fact "the de-historization and deculturation of subordinate peoples and the imposition of constructed identities have helped in the process of economic and political domination".[19]

Later this was translated into more pluralistic models,[20] that were more sensitive to the historical situations and the lived experience of peoples. This approach distanced itself from the deculturation and assimilation of ethnic diversity into an all-embracing hegemony, which was associated with the early liberals. However, these 'new ethnicists' and pluralists are, in the final analysis, a readaptation within, rather than a breakthrough out of the liberal tradition.

In classical Marxism ethnicity is subsumed under class divisions that are essentially economic differences, which have political consequences. But soon it became apparent, that the capitalist state rather than homogenizing ethnic differences within it, on the contrary "produces the condition for the rise of ethnic self-consciousness and accelerates parochial loyalties".[21] Later with neo-Marxism, ethnic differences are seen to be reinforced and to become "a mechanism for the recreation of hegemony and the reproduction of socio-economic inequality".[22] However, the Marxist approaches, still

> leave ethnicity unexplained, or explained as a vague superstructural phenomenon serving ruling class interests, ... to keep the workforce divided and preclude the development of class consciousness.[23]

The more recent civilizational or ethno-national approach developed in Latin America and Africa is opposed to both extremes: "to perspectives that maintain the autonomy of ethnicity and to economistic reductionism".[24] Rather it emphasizes both economic and socio-cultural domination, that gives rise to ethnic formations among the oppressed, but now "emerging peoples", who will have "a central role in the forging of a new society".[25]

However, this approach remains somewhat weak in locating ethnic movements within the class structure. Hence the distinction between an ethnicity that supports the dominant class hegemony, as in populist nationalist politics, and one that opposes this from the counter-hegemonic subalterns, is blurred if not lost. For ethnicity and class generally reinforce each other, for better or for worse. In India such multiple disadvantages most often add up to a "cumulative backwardness".[26] But such a "system of cumulative inequalities" does not automatically transform itself into one of "dispersed inequalities".[27] In fact "industrialization did not so much transform cumulative distribution of inequalities as intensify it".[28]

In view of this discussion, then, our approach to ethnicity must face the crucial issue of class consciousness and ethnic identity, not from any reductionist perspectives, whether this be eco-political or socio-cultural, but from one, that is inclusive of them.

ETHNICITY AND CLASS

Our understanding of ethnicity cannot remain preoccupied with delimiting its substantive core but must comprehend how an ethnic group articulates with the wider structures of social stratification, and how the group in turn gets stratified by these. For an ethnic group cannot be studied as an isolated, autonomous sub-system. This is certainly true of tribals in India today.

Tribe and Caste

Now tribal society is not hierarchically segregated. There is no sacred principle of ritual purity/pollution that stratifies, inter- or intra-tribal societies. The *Homo hierarchicus* of Louis Dumont is very far from 'tribal man'.[29] Yet it is an illusion to think of tribals as homogeneous peoples any more. They were always segmented into various tribes and increasingly today tribal society is stratified by class.

Some tribes have over time been sanskritized into the jati system. In this context it made sense to speak of a tribe-caste continuum. This of course assumes an assimilationist model. But for those who have kept their tribal identity and stayed out of the jati hierarchy this does not apply. But with a capitalist model of development, it would be hard to see how tribal society could resist the forces of class formation. Thus Pathy affirms that—

> without any exaggeration one can say that over 90 per cent of the so-called tribes are actually class societies inextricably intertwined with the Indian political economy as a whole.[30]

In practice "class consciousness develops out of the collectively experienced everyday reality".[31] A class-in-itself is not translated into a class-for-itself by some abstract discourse, but by lived common experiences. And "when ethnic ascription and class situation correlate,....both ethnic and class consciousness may develop in unison."[32] This can provide a powerful strategic basis for group mobilization. But when a big ethnic community is stratified by class divisions, or a large social class is segmented into many ethnic groups, then the contradictions between class and ethnic interests can be manipulated and mobilized by vested interests.

Tribal Minorities

Now whether these ethnic groups are mobilized to change or preserve the status quo would depend on whether they have subordinate or dominant social status. When an ethnic group is subordinate, then we have an 'ethnic minority'. Here there is an overlap between an ethnic identity that is socio-culturally subservient and a class status that is eco-politically subordinate. With tribes in India, especially the smaller ones, this coincidence of negative identity and low status is not unusual.

The Indian Constitution recognizes only linguistic and religious minorities, and the courts have defined a 50 per cent limit for a group to be considered a minority in a state. However, the term minority group as it is used today in the social sciences, does not refer to relative numbers. To quote the *International Encyclopedia of the Social Sciences:*

> Contemporary sociologists generally define a minority as ..... a group of people-differentiated from others in the same society by race, nationality, religion or language who both think of themselves as a differentiated group and are thought of by the others as a differentiated group with negative

> connotations. Further, they are relatively lacking in power and hence are subjected to certain exclusions, discriminations and other differential treatment.[33]

The essential features, then are not just some objective characteristics, but a subjective construct consisting of a set of attitudes: self-definition from within and prejudice from without; and a set of behaviours: self-segregation from within and discrimination and exclusion from without.[34]

Pathy rightly insists that "the Scheduled Tribes undisputedly possess all the properties of ethnic minorities".[35] But since we are referring to tribal ethnicity, we would prefer to be more specific with the term "tribal minorities". Whatever the terminology, the insistence on the class dimension of ethnicity is precisely to ensure that ethnic identities are not manipulated in favour of dominant group interests.

Manipulation and Mobilization

Such manipulation happens not just from without but from within tribal society as well. Here Ghanshyam Shah is worth quoting at some length. The better-off, more vocal tribals

> mobilize poor tribals whose class consciousness is subdued by talking euphemistically of 'tribal development' and 'tribal culture', or by raising issues of `tribal backwardness', 'injustice to tribals', etc.. The leaders of the vocal sections pressurize the government for more and more tribal development. Needless to say, this means the development of their own class in tribal society as against the poor Adivasis.... They are interested in seeing a middle or rich cultivator or an educated person from among them as a cabinet minister in the state, to get more reservations in white collar jobs, to organise cooperative banks which can support Adivasi entrepreneurs to get irrigation facilities, fertilizers, improved seeds and so on. They make these and other demands in the name of the Adivasis, but in practice, their concern for an ordinary Adivasis is not only secondary but also instrumental.[36]

Thus just as the better-off tribals are mobilized by the non-tribals for their own class interests, though they may later try to restrict or deny the tribals their share in the pay-off, so too are the poorer tribals mobilized by the better-off ones. This is possible precisely because

> the poor Adivasis are mobilized in politics by the vocal tribal on tribal and non-tribal rather than on class lines. Moreover, the vocal strata of the tribals instil 'tribalness' in terms tribal culture which tranquilizers the poor. But the vocal tribals themselves discard the so-called `tribal culture' in their day-to-day life because it is against their own aspiration and interests.[37]

Thus class inequalities of the larger society are reproduced with a tribal people through the use of ethnicity.

The hijacking of a mass movement or a people's struggle by an articulate and active elite to their own cause and interests is not unique to tribal mobilization. Too easily have poorer people involved in such movements allowed appeals to their ethnic identity to obfuscate the authentic concerns and interests of their class and/or minority status. Mobilizing a people on the basis of such an identity without reference to class relations, makes possible, and indeed invites just this. Populist appeals to 'national honour and integrity' community or group 'unity and harmony', etc., rarely raise the question of who pays the price of such honour and integrity, who carries the burden for such unity and harmony. For seldom is it the vocal elites, making such appeals, who do.

The Indigenous Myth

In this context the International Labour Organisation's (ILO) Convention 169 of 1989 "Concerning Indigenous and Tribal Peoples in Independent Countries" may have done the best it could at the time. But it still leaves much to be desired. For it identifies 'tribal peoples' in terms of "social, cultural and economic conditions" which distinguish them from the other sections of the national community (Art 1: 1. 1), and indigenous peoples' in terms of "their descent from the populations which inhabited the country, or a geographical region at the time of conquest or colonization or the establishment of present state boundaries", who retain their "social, economic, cultural and political institutions" (Art 1. 1. b). However, it still affirms that—

> self-identification as indigenous or tribal shall be regarded as a fundamental criterion for determining the groups to

> which the provisions of this convention apply. (Art 1.2.)

Although there is an informal understanding that 'indigenous' covers isolated and marginal peoples, the official documentation adds up to a rather weak reference to the economic and political aspects that are essential to the class structure. And while in the Americas and Australia given their colonial history it may be easy to identify 'indigenous and tribal peoples', in India this can be far more problematic. Already there are apprehensions that the Indian Council of Indigenous and Tribal Peoples (ICITP), formed on the initiative of a one time deputy minister in the Central Government, has an effective membership, that "is confined to a few significant personalities of the Chotanagpur region".[38]

Dalits too have begun claiming indigenous status in this country, and non-minority groups have done the same as well. Thus the Dravidian movement in the south which began in the 1920s with the Justice Party of the backward castes would see the Dravidians as the original inhabitants of the subcontinent, much before the conquering Aryans arrived.

More recently the forward castes in the north with the Hindutva movement have begun claiming indigenous status for the Aryans![39] The ominous implications of such claims are that only the religious minorities, except for the indigenous religions, like Buddhism, Jainism, Sikhism, would be non-indigenous and therefore alien! We must of course ask: who pays the price and who gets the pay-off for such religious nationalism in India today? The chauvinistic manipulation of such religious identities only shows to what extremes this can go of when the class dimension is swept away.

More than just cautioning against religious fanaticism, our purpose here is to point to the darker more dangerous side of the "Myth of Indigenous People". For specially—

> where historical memory is short, the idea of 'indigenous people' provides abundant scope for the proliferation of myths relating to blood and soil.[40]

Our century has witnessed the cry of 'blut und boden' raised by those who precipitated a genocide and a World War. Alarmingly, some in this country, who do not seem to have learnt anything from that holocaust, may be condemned to repeat it. Already we are witnessing a brutal and bloody "ethnic cleansing" in some parts of the world, which has a menacing echo in the recent events here with the surge of orchestrated communal violence, that has errupted through the country.

Ethnicity as Process

In sum then, there is a plurality of ethnic discourses, because there is a complexity in ethnic expressions, since "ethnicity should be conceived as a process evolving through time".[41] Moreover,

> in the hands of the state and the dominant classes, ethnicity serves as an element to reproduce systems of social relationships, to validate structures of inequality and to support policies of social control.[42]

However, with marginalized minorities,

> on the other hand, ethnic consciousness may provide the foundations for the emergence of an oppositional consciousness, expressed in counter-hegemonic practices.[43]

The difference between the two is precisely in the way ethnicity as a process articulates with the class structure. Our caution here has been against its actual manipulation by dominant groups, our concern is for its potential in mobilizing subordinate ones. Certainly, a static understanding of group identity can by itself do little to break the status quo; and an atavistic romanticising of an indigenous or tribal one cannot by itself create a class consciousness. But a dynamically constructed ethnic identity can mobilize a group consciousness responsive to the realities of the eco-political structures and make an ethnic group-in-itself, a socio-economic class-in-itself as well. This is to us the crux of the issue in addressing the of tribal minority status.

TRIBAL INTEGRATION

Tribal minorities, as we have explained, are distinctive ethnic groups in a subordinate class position. The issue to be addressed in their regard is one of overcoming their minority status and affirming their tribal identity, or rather remedying the first by mobilizing the second. In other words, integrating tribal people into a culturally pluralist, economically egalitarian society, and not assimilating them into an ethnically uniform, class-stratified state. But integration has not always been the official policy with regard to our tribals nor has it been understood in the same way by all concerned or at different times.

Isolation and Assimilation

In the colonial period there was a policy of isolation, but this was not in fact effective. The needs of the colonial state, its paternalism notwithstanding, were often satisfied at the cost of the tribals. The many tribal revolts, and even more so their forcible suppression, is ample evidence of this. The deteriorating terms of exchange between the tribals and the outside world epitomizes the relationship between the two: neither autonomous isolation nor egalitarian integration, but a deculturated assimilation at the lower end of the class strata that were being formed wherever the colonial political economy penetrated.

Today it is no longer possible for tribals to retreat into isolation, even if this were desirable, which we think not. For this approach to the tribals seems to assume a static identity, often idealized by non-tribals.

Among the Indian anthropologists, who urged the tribals' entry into the national mainstream, many have advocated their assimilation into non-tribal society, much the same way as the 'Hindu mode of absorption' did earlier. Thus Ghurye would want an "integrative assimilation", that would make the tribals "part and parcel of the Hindu Indian polity that is slowly but surely arising",[44] and he would want tribal languages, which tend "to counter-balance to some extent the speeding up of the process of assimilation",[45] replaced by the Indo-Aryan languages.[46] There are others, who would not go along with such a 'Hinduization' of the tribals, but would still want to "give up the idea of integration altogether and think of helping the tribals to detribalize themselves" so as to be indistinguishable from other people in the region.[47]

What the assimilationists seem to suggest, then, is overcoming tribal minority status by sacrificing their ethnic identity. But our experience in the field is contrary to this. For one thing the potential of a positive identity to mobilize the group is lost, and the process of assimilation leaves the tribals with a negative self-image and a deteriorating socio-economic status.

Integration and Identity

Since Independence the Government of India's tribal policy has not been assimilationist but it has tried to follow the 'panchsheel' proposed by Nehru in 1959. However, the development it has pursued has been more disintegrative for the tribals than a genuine integration, with internal autonomy and economic equity.

For, as a group of eminent scholars at a seminar on "The Tribal Situation in India" asserted in their concluding statement:

> integration must be sharply distinguished from assimilation which means complete loss of cultural identity for the weaker groups.... integration is a dynamic process which necessarily involves mutual give-and-take by the various sections of the national community.[48]

Integration, then, depends very much on what kind of society our tribals are being integrated into. Is it the caste hierarchy of our traditional culture, or the class stratification precipitated by our present political economy, or the pluralist-secular, democratic-socialist ideal sketched in our Constitution? It is only this last that can accommodate the kind of tribal integration we envisage, one which will salvage both their identity and dignity.

For in the caste hierarchy integration must mean a loss of their tribal identity, in a class system they are only confirmed in their minority status. And yet, since caste is very much a factor to be reckoned with in our culture, just as class is in our economy, any realistic approach to integration must take cognisance of both these.

The Tribal Contribution

Hence a dynamic process of tribal integration must not only preserve their cultural autonomy, but also mobilize them to participate in their own development, which in turn must be both equitable and sustainable. Needless to say, it is the smaller, poorer tribes that are most in need of such development and most deprived of it too. But, if dynamic integration is also to be a two-way process, in which tribal dignity and identity is respected and preserved, then it must be sensitive to their contribution to the larger society as well. This has not always been conceded so here we mention only a few convincing instances.

With regard to sustainable development of forests and other eco-sensitive regions, Gadgil and Guha point to two paradoxes, with regard to the ecological impact of different modes of resource use[49]: the greater the distance, of the users from the resource the greater the ecological impact; the faster the development of scientific knowledge, the greater the environmental degradation. It would seem obvious that the people who live close to and accept their dependence on the environment are better able to live in harmony with it, than those who want only to exploit it from a distance for commercial purposes. Indeed, in marginal lands,

> unlike tribal societies, both agro-industrial groups and peasant farmers have shown themselves almost totally unable to manage sustainably and produce effectively in such environments.[50]

Moreover, in preserving the precious and precarious bio-diversity of the planet, "indigenous knowledge is essential for the use, identification, and cataloging of the biota".[51] What our tribals do represent

> therefore, is a significant economic opportunity for the nation, not a luxury. They are at the forefront of knowledge of the management of marginal environments and can contribute to the national society. Sustainable exploitation of eco-systems often considered marginal is becoming increasingly necessary for national societies and the world as a whole. Capitalization on these unique strengths is highly desirable for economic development.[52]

It might seem ironic, but it is now becoming more apparent though still somewhat reluctantly admitted in conventional circles, that given their accumulated experience and collective traditions, tribal—

> religion and custom as ideologies of resource use are perhaps better adapted to deal with a situation of imperfect, knowledge than a supposedly 'scientific' resource management.[53]

Our frantic pursuit of an ever higher 'standard of living', has not lead to a corresponding improvement in our 'quality of life', but has rather compromised and even undermined it. Such contradictions challenge us to a new understanding of development in which we have much to learn from tribal societies, especially with regard to a cultural basis for a sustainable relationship to our environment.

The Tribal Challenge

However, it is not only at the margin or the periphery of a society that tribals have an important and valuable contribution to make. For tribal non-consumerist solidarity provides an alternative to the competitive, consumerism of the non-tribal world. This is a moral challenge we cannot afford to ignore, in view of the pervading crises which have riddled our society.

Redfield and Singer have explained how the development of urbanization homogenizes society by coordinating and systematizing "the norms provided by the Great Traditions", together with "the weakening or supersession of the local and traditional cultures".[54] When, social crises demand change, it is the `little tradition', which has not become inert, that in fact

> may retain a greater vitality and disposition to change than the systematized Great Tradition that gets 'located' in special classes and urban centers.[55]

Often enough it is these marginal groups that have posed a substantial challenge for a revitalization and regeneration of the larger society. Here it may well be the distinctive cultural traits of a tribal group rather than its relative size and influence that may pose the more incisive question, the moral challenge to the 'other' in us in search for an alternative way of life. For in spite of the apparent difference and distance between these two worlds, there is the real possibility of creative communication. For "in every tribal settlement there is civilization; in every city is the folk society".[56]

Indeed, at a deeper level, the tribal nomad in the forest-hills may have more relevance to George Simmel's 'Stranger' in the metropolitan cities,[57] than may appear superficially at first.

Strategies for Action

In attempting, then, an integrative response to the fundamental issues of the tribal question, we do not pretend to come up with neat recipes and time bound programmes. However, we can now bring/draw together the various stands on our discussion and attempt to stretch the general outlines of such a response.

If the unequal exchange that marginalizes these tribals is to be reversed, then, they must not be left in isolation, not even in the mistaken notion of preserving their tribal identity. This only marginalize them still further. For we have seen that ethnic identity a dynamic, not a static concept, and precisely because of this, can be mobilized to create a people's movement. Once we accept this then, the real issue is not preserving a static culture, but rather one of promoting a cultural autonomy, that will allow them to redefine their identity, without in anyway further compromising their dignity. It is their human dignity that must become the focal point of constituting a dynamic tribal identity and the integrating axis of their response to redressing their minority status.

For, if the downward spiral in which the tribals are caught, is to be reversed, then, the very developmental model that we are pursuing and into which we want to integrate them, needs to be challenged. Our unwillingness to do this, adds up to a refusal to face the tribal question in any depth. It is precisely such a refusal that will not only compromise the tribals, but marginalize all disadvantaged group, as well, and eventually negate our vision of a just and equitable society itself. And yet this very commitment to integrate such diverse but disadvantaged groups into our society can force us to question and reorient our development process sooner rather than later.

However any effective action strategy to mobilize tribal ethnicity, must be careful not to negate or fight shy of class consciousness. This will make the tribal response broader based by bringing it into alliance with similarly placed disadvantaged groups in our society. It will also prevent tribal movements from fragmenting themselves into their different component tribes or getting stratified into a classes across and within the tribe itself.

This is precisely the danger against which this study would caution, since we already have seen an intimation of something similar in backward caste móvements that have time and again in specific instances turned hostile to the scheduled and other lower caste groups. The inability of tribal leaders to put together a sustained and unified tribal movement in the country, is also evidence of stronger tribal sub-identities being manipulated against the larger interest of the tribals themselves, whether consciously or unconsciously.

What exactly the contours of such a tribal movement will be, it is not clear now, and certainly not for an outsider, or non-tribal to attempt to put this together prematurely. However, if the general direction of a viable movement is to be chartered, or indicated, then our conclusions would seem to point to the need for mobilizing a dynamic and adaptive tribal identity, with a class consciousness that will redress their minority status, and forge linkages with similarly disadvantaged groups.

For this they must demand a cultural autonomy, which has for no long been effectively denied, as well as a reversal of the unequal exchange relationship, which have till now marginalized and exploited them. Together this will have the potential of questioning our models of growth and contributing to a new paradigm of development. In fact the response our society gives to the tribal question, will be a touchstone of the authenticity of its own democratic integration.

MARGINALIZATION AND RESPONSE

A concluding reflection to this monograph will attempt to respond to the more specific situation of the Kathkaris in the light of the more general analysis we have made. We must now ask: how it is possible to redress their class status, and not at the same time sacrifice their ethnic identity? Our urging here is that ethnic identity be mobilized to empower people to resist their marginalization, and to struggle for a more equitable distributive justice. The difficulty, however, as we have remarked earlier, is that for a marginalized people, their sense of self-worth is correspondingly affected, as also is their ethnic identity and pride.

As a small marginalised tribe in a rapidly developing district, the Kathkaris are all the more vulnerable to the changes engulfing them. But precisely for this reason, they provide us with a critical test at a crucial point in our developmental process. Will they be steamrolled by the juggernaut of development, or will they survive, and how? The answer to this will be indicative of how our society is responding to the fundamental issues we have raised in the first chapter of this monograph: equity, sustainability, participation, autonomy, integration.

Our reconstruction of the Kathkari profile in chapter three, established that the Kathkaris were able to adapt and adjust to changing circumstances all through their history, right up to colonial period, without being assimilated into the local jati system. In preserving their distinctive identity, they were also able to affirm a positive, yet critical self-image and preserve a sense of self-worth, that sustained them in being somewhat more active subjects, rather than passive objects in the changes they were undergoing as a community.

It was only when the colonial government began to cut off the sustaining alternative which the forest provided to these forest dwellers, that the terms of exchange between them and the outside world began to deteriorate. The unequal terms of the exchange, which they were subjected to, could not but eventually lead to their exploitation and marginalization, and to their eventual degradation even! For with the material basis of their tribal culture destroyed, their way of life could not be maintained.

Our post-independence policy has attempted to reverse this downward spiral, with a protective discrimination for scheduled castes and tribes as also for other disadvantage groups. However, the performance of the government in the field, in implementing such policies, has left much to be desired.

Kathkari Identity and Mobilization

Yet in our analysis of the present situation, in which the Kathkaris of this district find themselves, we perceive new orientations emerging, that need to be supported and strengthened and built into a people's movement. They are now much more aware of the exploitation, to which they are subjected, as their demands for land, fair wages, and education for their children indicate. In their desire to join the main stream, they recognize the need to adapt and change their way of life. In fact, we notice that they want to be identified more by their economic class status and not only by their ethnic tribal community.

What seems to be paradoxical, but is not really so, is that our top-down process of development has not really led to an ethnic homogeneity, but only to increased marginalization of minority groups. For what in fact has happened is that dominant groups have used a sense of group identity to mobilize themselves and take advantage of the developmental process, while subordinate ones have been left on the periphery with, not just a changed, but rather a declining sense of group identity. In such circumstances it is difficult for a group to find a solidarity for themselves based on their ethnicity. This is precisely the kind of self-alienation and anomie in which marginalization results.

Contrary to the 'modernization' that our top-down planning was supposed to bring, what in fact has trickled down are not the real advantages of development, but only the left-over crumbs. In this process ethnic groups at the margin of our society are assimilated and then subordinated at the bottom of our social strata.

Our investigations have found that the Kathkaris in this district do in fact respond positively do the initiatives taken by various agencies in the field. But it is precisely the agencies that act, not so much on their behalf, but initiate a process of bottom up change with them, that are the ones best able to mobilize and empower these tribals. The kind of solidarity that is often evoked by such movements, has not been exclusively restricted to tribal identity. Rather it is open to other similar economically disadvantaged groups as well. In fact for the Kathkaris themselves, their group identity seems to be now crystallizing along the class dimension as they increasingly come to see themselves as 'adivasi' and distance themselves from which we have seen is interpreted with strong economic nuances, their older tribal identity as 'Kathkaris'.

In fact, it would be difficult to sustain the momentum of their movement, without forging links with other groups on a class rather than a caste or ethnic basis.[58] In other words, here too class status cannot be ignored, in favour of ethnic identity.

With the smaller tribal groups, like the Kathkaris, the danger would seem to be, that an overemphasis on their ethnic identity may isolate them and prevent them from forging links of solidarity with other similarly disadvantaged groups. The danger with much larger groups might be otherwise, that is, as we have pointed out earlier in this chapter, the ethnic identity of the group is mobilized without reference to class, and consequently results in an intra-tribal stratification, with the better off tribals in the group taking advantages of the changes and leaving the poorer ones behind.

Habitats: Old and New

It might appear, however, that, the Kathkari culture has little to contribute to the rapidly industrializing district of Raigad. But when it comes to a sustainable relationship with the environment there, they do represent a significant challenge. For if the Kathkaris are to survive this process of development, then a significant factor surely will be the regeneration of the forest in these areas. Vast tracts of land here are neither suitable for agriculture nor industrialization, since the area is hilly. Experience has shown that it is the forest dwellers who eventually are the best caretakers and protectors of the forest, and so integrating the Kathkaris into a process of afforestation would in fact be restoring the forest dwellers to their original habitat.

But the forest will not be the only alternative available for these tribals. They are already making their way into settled agriculture as farmers, and also into the urban industrial centres as workers. Here too it is important for them to have some sense of ethnic identity and pride to share themselves up against the inevitable alienation that people, especially the poorer, weaker sections, are subject to in the lonely, 'madding crowd' of our mass society.

However, it is not our intention to romanticize the tribal way of life. Rather we believe that like every human identity, tribal ethnic identity too must be dynamic and actualize the human potential that is present in every human group. The danger however, in romanticizing them is to condemn them to a primitivism, that we ourselves are only too reluctant to embrace, except in the security of our academic fantasies!

The correspondence we have established between a negative ethnic identity and a marginalized social status is crucial for any interventionist strategy that seeks to empower people to break out of the poverty trap. For tribals, as we have seen, this implies integration in the larger society, but not necessarily with a loss of their distinctiveness.

Precisely in keeping their identity will they make their special contribution to the mainstream society, and challenge it to a deeper human authenticity. But by isolating the tribals we stymie both, their contribution and their challenge to our society. Perhaps this is not entirely an indeliberate way of coping with the unsettling 'other', the outsider, the stranger, whose 'design for living', is in so many ways is contrapuntal to our mainstream way of life.

Vavilovian Centres and the Tribal Dilemma

There is an intriguing image that comes to mind when we confront the dilemma that the tribal question poses for us.

Ecologists have come to realize that bio-diversity is the best guarantor of survival. This applies to the genetic pool of a species, as also to the species within a 'biome', or biotic area. For as commercially exploited species, like mass produced agricultural crops, become more and more uniform to meet the increasingly standardized preferences of a mass market there is a corresponding uniformity and loss of diversity in the genetic pool of the seed. This makes it highly vulnerable to mutant strains of pests and virus and parasites, its natural enemies, that attack it. The genetically designed species becomes increasingly vulnerable to the mutant predator. In other words, these species becomes less resilient and more vulnerable, to the environment. Mono-cropping only accentuates this danger even further, putting at risk not only the species, but the whole biotic area as well.

To regenerate the species to cope with its changed environment one has to go back to the original genetic home where the species still survives in the wild. These are called Vavilovian centres, after the Russian scientist, Nikolai Ivanovich Valvilov, who first discovered and described them.[59] The genetic pool is richer here, and genes, resistant to the new pestilence can be identified and spliced into the enfeebled crop to make it vigorous and marketable once again.

If we assimilate the tribals into our society, we do away with any possible contribution or challenge they may be able to make to our society as tribals, and though we may devalue their contribution now, are we sure we will never be in need of it in the future? And if we leave them isolated, 'natural, wild and free', are we not freezing them into a time-warp as 'objects' to be 'used' by us, if and when we need them?

The response we are urging here is to reject both these alternatives. For we do value the contribution and challenge they make to us already now. Our unsustainable, polluting consumerist society needs this constructive critique from a counter-cultural 'other'. Assimilation or isolation of our tribals cannot do this.

What we must struggle for together with our tribals, then, is to achieve an integration that will address the fundamental issues of the tribal question, issues that concern all ethnic minorities in our country as well: social equity, ecological sustainability, people's participation, cultural autonomy and democratic integration. If we are pointing to a utopia which is many giant leaps out of our reach just yet, then we can at least begin to grasp, what the small steps are that we must take already now to make a more integrative response to the larger tribal dilemma.

REFERENCES

1. K. S. Singh, *Tribal Society in India, op. cit.*, p. 254.
2. *ibid.*, Cf. Jaganath Pathy, "An Outline of Modes of Production, in `Tribal India'", in B. Chaudhuri, ed., *Tribal Development in India, op. cit.*, pp. 23-48.
3. Susana B. C. Devalle, *Discourses of Ethnicity: Culture and Protest in Jarkhand*, Sage Pub., New Delhi, 1992, p. 33.
4. J. Pathy, *Ethnic Minorities op. cit.*, p. 195.
5. S. B. C. Devalle, *op. cit.*, p. 31.
6. Surajit Sinha, "Tribe-Caste and Peasant-Caste Continua in Central India," *Man in India*, 1965, Vol. 45., No.1, pp. 57-83.
7. S. C. Dube, *Tribal Heritage in India, I: Ethnicity, Identity and Interaction*, Vikas, New Delhi, 1977, pp. 1-5.
8. S. B. C. Devalle, *op. cit.*, p. 16.
9. *ibid.*, p. 18.
10. Cf. J.Pathy, *Ethnic Minorities, op. cit.*, pp. 4-5.
11. Benedict Anderson, *Imagined Communities: Reflections on the Origin and Spread of Nationalism*, Verso, London, 1983.
12. E. J. Hobsbawm and T. O. Ranger, eds. *The Invention of Traditions*, Cambridge University Press, Cambridge, 1983.
13. S. B. C. Devalle, *op. cit.*, p. 18.
14. J. Pathy, Ethnic Minorities, *op. cit.*, p.19.
15. Clifford Geertz, ed., *Old Societies and New States*, Free Press, New York, 1963.
16. Fredrik Barth, ed., *Ethnic Groups and Boundaries: The Social Organisation of Culture Difference*, George Allen and Unwin, London, 1970.
17. S. Lyman and N. A. Douglas "Ethnicity: Strategies of Collective and Individual Impression Management", *Social Research*, Vol. 40, No.2, 1973 pp.344-65.
18. D. Handelman, "The Organisation of Ethnicity", *Ethnic Groups*, Vol.I, No.3, 1977, pp. 187-200.
19. S. B. C. Devalle, *op. cit.*, p. 28.
20. Cf. F. Barth, ed., *op. cit.*, and Clifford Geertz, *The Interpretation of Cultures*, Basic Books, New York, 1973.
21. J. Pathy, *Ethnic Minorities, op. cit.*, p. 6.
22. S. B. C. Devalle, *op. cit.*, p. 43.
23. *ibid.*, p. 44.
24. *ibid.*, p. 45.
25. *ibid.*, p. 46.
26. Marc Galanter, *Competing Equalities: Law and the Backward Classes in India*, Oxford University Press, Delhi, 1984, p.240.

27. Cf. Robert A. Dahl, *Who Governs? Democracy and Power in an American City*, Yale Univ. Press, New Haven, 1961, pp.85-6.
28. Robert A. Dahl, *Authority in a Good Society: After the Revolution*, Allied Pub., Bombay, 1972, p. 109.
29. Louis Dumont, *Homo Hierarchicus: The Caste System and its Implications*, Weidenfeld and Nicolson, London, 1970.
30. J. Pathy, *Ethnic Minorities, op. cit.*, p. 29.
31. S. B. C. Devalle, *op. cit.*, p. 238.
32. *ibid.*
33. Arnold M. Rose, "Minorities", in David L. Sills, ed., *International Encyclopedia of the Social Sciences*, Vol. 10, Macmillan, New York, 1968, pp. 365-70.
34. Cf. *ibid.*
35. J. Pathy, *Ethnic Minorities, op. cit.*, p. 194.
36. Ghanshyam Shah, "Tribal Identity and Class Differentiations: A Case Study of the Chaudhuri Tribe", in Dipankar Gupta, ed., *Social Stratification*, Oxford University Press, Delhi, 1991, p.301.
37. *ibid.*
38. B. K. Roy Burman, "Indigenous and Tribal Peoples: Global Hegemonies and Government of India", *Mainstream*, Vol. 30, No.46, 5th September 1992, p 33 , (pp. 31-5).
39. Cf. Srikant G. Telageri, *The Aryan Invasion Theory and Indian Nationalism*, Aditya Prakashan, New Delhi, 1993.
40. Andre Beteille, "Myth of Indigenous People: Dark Face of a Popular Belief", *Times of India*, New Delhi, 5th January 1993, p. 8.
41. S. B. C. Devalle, *op. cit.*, p.18.
42. *ibid.*, p.239.
43. *ibid.*, p.240.
44. G.S. Ghurye, *op. cit.*, p. 211.
45. *ibid.*, p.152.
46. *ibid.*, p.190.
47. Gouranga Chatlopadhya, "The Problem of Tribal Integration to Urban Industrial Society: A Theoretical Approach", in K. Suresh Singh, ed., *The Tribal Situation in India*, Indian Institute of Advanced Studies, Shimla, 1972, p. 491, pp. 486-93.
48. K. Suresh Singh, ed., *The Tribal Situation in India: Proceedings of a Seminar, op. cit.*, "Statement Issued by the Seminar", pp. 631-2.
49. Gadgil and Guha, *op. cit.*, p.52.
50. Robert Goodland, *op. cit.*, p. 13.
51. *ibid.*, p.14.
52. *ibid.*, p. 15.
53. Gadgil and Guha, *op. cit.*, p. 53.
54. Robert Redfield and Milton B. Singer, "City and Countryside: The Cultural Independence", in Teodor Shanin, ed., *Peasants and Peasant Societies: Selected Readings*, Penguin, Middlesex, England, 1971, p. 349, pp. 337-65.
55. *ibid.* p.359.
56. *ibid.* p. 343.
57. Cf. P. Levine, ed., *Individuality and Social Forms*, University of Chicago Press, Chicago, 1971, p. 143.
58. Cf. S. D. Kulkarni, "Class and Caste in a Tribal Movement", *Economic and Political Weekly*, Vol. 24, Nos. 7 and 8, Feb. 1979, pp. 465-8.
59. Cf. Al Gore, The Earth in Balance: Ecology and the Humans Spirit, Penguin, New York, 1993, pp. 131.

BIBLIOGRAPHY

Anderson, Benedict. *Imagined Communities: Reflections on the Origin and Spread of Nationalism,* Verso, London, 1983.

Barth, Fredrik (ed.) *Ethnic Groups and Boundaries: The Social Organisation of Culture Difference,* George Allen and Unwin, London, 1970.

Beteille, Andre. "Myth of Indigenous People Dark Face of a Popular Belief", *Times of India,* 5 January 1993.

——. *Society and Politics in India,* Oxford University Press, Delhi, 1992.

Bose, N.K. *Culture and Society in India,* Asia Publishing House, Bombay, 1967.

Campbell, J. M. *Bombay Gazetteer,* Vol. XI., Kolaba-Janjira, Government Central Press, Bombay, 1870.

Chandra, Bipan. et. al., *India's Struggle for Independence, 1857-1947,* Viking, New Delhi, 1988.

Chattopadhya, Gouranga. "The Problem of Tribal Integration to Urban Industrial Society: A Theoretical Approach", in K. S. Singh (ed.), *The Tribal Situation in India,* Indian Institute of Advanced Studies, Shimla, 1972.

Chatterji, Suniti Kumar. "The Indo-Mongoloids: Their Contributions to the History and Culture of India", *Royal Asiatic Society of Bengal,* Calcutta, 1951.

Chaubey, N.P. (ed). *Tribal Techniques, Social Organisation and Development: Disruption and Alternatives,* Indian Academy of Social Sciences, Allahabad, 1983.

Chaudhuri, Buddhadeb (ed), *Tribal Development in India: Problems and Prospectus,* Inter-India Pub., New Delhi, 1990, 2nd Edition.

——. (ed). *Tribal Transformation in India* (5 Vols), Inter-India Pub., New Delhi, 1992, Vols. I - V.

Dahl, Robert A. *Who Governs? Democracy and Power in an American City,* Yale Univ. Press, New Haven, 1961.

——. *Authority in a Good Society: After the Revolution,* Allied Pub., Bombay, 1972.

Danda, Ajit K. "Economic Transformation of Tribals in India", in Buddhadeb Chaudhuri, ed., *Tribal Development in India, op. cit.*

Deogaonkar, S.G. *Tribal Development Plans: Implementation and Evaluation,* Concept Pub., New Delhi, 1992.

Desai, A.R. "Tribes in Transition", in Buddhadeb Chaudhuri (ed.), *Tribal Development in India, op. cit.*.

Devalle, Susana B.C. *Discourses of Ethnicity: Culture and Protest in Jarkhand,* Sage Pub., New Delhi, 1992.

Doshi, S.L. *Tribal Ethnicity, Class and Integration,* Rawat Pub., Jaipur, 1990.

Dube, S.C. Approaches to the Tribal Problem in India, in L. P. Vidyarthi (ed.), *op.cit.*.

——. "Inaugurate Address", in K.S. Singh (ed.) *The Tribal Situation in India, op. cit.*.

——. *Tribal Heritage in India, I: Ethnicity, Identity and Interaction,* Vikas, New Delhi, 1977.

Dumont, Louis. *Homo Hierarchicus: The Caste System and its Implications,* Weidenfeld and Nicolson, London, 1970.

Elwin, Verrier. *Philosophy for NEFA* (2nd ed.), Govt. of Assam, Shillong 1959.

——. *The Baiga,* John Murray, London, 1939.

Evans, Pritchard E.E. et al.. *The Institutions of Primitive Society: A Series of Broadcast Talks,* Godfref Lienhardf, Basil Blackwell, Oxford, 1954.

Forsyth, J. *The Highlands of Central India,* Chapman and Hall, London, 1889.

Frank, Andre Gunder. *Development of Underdevelopment,* Monthly Review Press, New York.

Fuchs, Stephen. *The Aboriginal Tribes of India,* Macmillan India, Delhi, 1973.

——. *Rebellious Prophets: A Study of Messianic Movements in Indian Religious,* Asia Pub. House, Bombay, 1965.

——. "The Religion of Indian Tribals", in Buddhadeb Chaudhuri (ed.), *Tribal Development, op. cit.,* Vol. V.

Gagdil, Madhav and Ramachandra Guha. *This Fissured Land: An Ecological History of India,* Oxford University Press, Delhi, 1992.

Galanter, Marc. *Competing Equalities: Law and the Backward Classes in India,* Oxford University Press, Delhi, 1984.

Geertz, Clifford. (ed.). *Old Societies and New States,* Free Press, New York, 1963.

——. *The Interpretation of Cultures,* Basic Books, New York, 1973.

Gellner, Ernest. *Culture, Identity and Politics,* Cambridge University Press, Cambridge, 1987.

Ghurye, G.S. *The Scheduled Tribes,* Popular Prakashan, Bombay, third edition, 1963.

Gisbert, Pascual. Preliterate Man: A Synthetic View of 'Primitive Man', *Manaktalas,* Bombay, 1967.

Godelier, M. *Perspectives in Marxist Anthropology,* Cambridge Univ. Press, London, 1977.

Goodland, Robert. *Tribal Peoples and Economic Development; Human Ecologic Considerations,* World Bank, Washington, 1982.

Gore, Al. *The Earth in Balance: Ecology and the Humans Spirit,* Penguin, New York, 1993.

Handelman, D. "The Organisation of Ethnicity", *Ethnic Groups,* Vol.I, No.3, 1977, pp. 187-200.

Handoo, Jawaharlal. "Far From Truth: Anthropology and Tribal Studies", in Buddhadeb Chaudhuri (ed.), *Tribal Transformation in India, op. cit..*

Hardiman, David. *The Coming of the Devi: Adivasi Assertion in Western India,* Oxford University Press, Delhi, 1987.

Hardy, G.J. *Gazetteer of The Bombay Presidency,* Vol XI-B, Kolaba and Janjira, Government Central Press, Bombay, 1913.

——. *Gazetteer of the Bombay Presidency,* Volume XI-B. Kolaba and Janjira. Government Central Press, Bombay, 1921.

——. *Primary Census Abstract.* Office of The Director of Census, Maharashtra, Bombay, 1991.

Harris, Marvin. *Cultural Materialism: The Struggle for a Science of Culture,* Random House, New York, 1980.

Heredia, Rudolf, C. *Voluntary Action and Development: Towards a Praxis for Non Government Agencies,* Concept, New Delhi, 1988.

Hobsbawm, E.J. and T. O. Ranger, eds. *The Invention of Traditions,* Cambridge University Press, Cambridge, 1983.

Kennedy, M. *The Criminal Classes in India,* Mittal Pub., Delhi, 1985.

Kosambi, D.D. *The Culture and Civilization of Ancient India in Historical Outline,* Routledge and Kegan Paul, London, 1965.

——. *An Introduction to the Study of Indian History,* Popular Prakashan, Bombay, 1975.

Kulkarni, S.D. "Class and Caste in a Tribal Movement", *Economic and Political Weekly,* Vol.14, No.7 & 8, Feb. 4979, pp. 465-8.

Levi-Strauss, Claude. "Anthropology: Its Achievements and Future", *Current Anthropology,* 1966, Vol.7, pp. 124-7.

Levine, P. (ed.). *Individuality and Social Forms,* University of Chicago Press, Chicago, 1971.

Lewis, I.M. "Tribal Society", in David L. Sills, ed. *International Encyclopedia of the Social Sciences,* Macmillan, New York, 1968, Vols.15, 16, 17.

Lyman, S. and N. A. Douglas. "Ethnicity: Strategies of Collective and Individual Impression Management", *Social Research,* Vol. 40, No.2, 1973, pp. 344-65.

Mandelbanm, D.G. *Society in India,* Popular Prakashan, Bombay, 1970.

Mann, R.S. "Economic Systems of Western Indian Tribes", in K.S. Singh ed., *The Tribal Situation in India, op.cit.,* 1992.

Marx, Karl and F. Engels. *Pre-Capitalist Socio-Economic Formations,* Progress Pub., Moscow, 1979.

Mehta, Piarey Lal. *Constitutional Protection to Scheduled Tribes in India in Retrospect and Prospect,* H.K. Publishers and Distributors, Delhi, 1991.

Meillasson, Claude. "From Reproduction to Production: A Marxist Approach to Economic Anthropology", *Economy and Society,* Vol. I, No. I, 1972, pp. 93-105.

Naik, T.B. "What is a Tribe? Conflicting Definitions", in *Applied Anthropology,* ed., L. P. Vidyarthi, Kitab Mahal, Allahabad, 1968,

Nandy, Ashish. *The Intimate Enemy: Loss and Recovery of Self Under Colonialism,* Oxford University Press, Delhi, 1983.

Pathy, Jaganath. *Ethnic Minorities in the Process of Development,* Rawat Pub., Jaipur, 1988.

— —. *Tribal Peasantry: Dynamics of Development,* Inter-India Publication, New Delhi, 1984.

Postan, M.M. *The Historical Method in Social Science,* The University Press, Cambridge, England, 1939.

Redfield, Robert. *The Little Community: Viewpoints for the Study of a Human Whole,* Univ. of Chicago Press, Chicago, 1962.

——. *The Primitive World and its Transformation,* Great Seas Books, Cornell Univ. Press, Ithara, New York, 1953.

Ribas Anthony S.J. *A Socio-Economic Survey of the Kune Mission, Part I.,* Social Welfare Centre, Kune, Khandala, P.O. Pune, Dist. Lonavala. P.O.412, Maharashtra, unpublished report, 1976.

——. *Socio-economic Survey of the Kune Mission—Part I,* unpublished report, 1976.

Rose, Arnold M. "Minorities", in David L. Sills, ed., *International Encyclopedia of the Social Sciences,* Vol. 10, Macmillan, New York, 1968, pp. 365-70.

Roy, Burman B.K. "Indigenous and Tribal Peoples, Global Hegemonies and Government of India", *Mainstream,* Vol.30, No.46, 5 Sep. 92, pp. 31-5.

——. "Issues in Tribal Development", in B. Chaudhuri, ed., *Tribal Transformation in India, op. cit.,* Vol. II.

——. "Persistence of Folk Law in India with Particular Reference to Tribal Communities", in Buddhadeb Chaudhuri, ed., *Tribal Transformation in India, op. cit..*

Sahlins D. Marshall and E. R. Service. *Evolution and Culture,* University of Michigan Press, Ann Arbor, 1960.

Sengupta, Nirmal. "Reappearising Tribal Movements I: A Myth in the Making", *Economic and Political Weekly,* Vol.23, No.19, 7 May 1988, pp. 943-5. pt. II, *ibid.,* No.20, 14 May 1988, pp. 1003-05, pt.III, *ibid.,* No.21, 21 May 1988, pp. 1054-5.

Shah, Ghanshyam. "Tribal Identity and Class Differentiations: A Caste Study of the Chandhari Tribe", in Dipankar Gupta, ed., *Social Stratification,* Oxford Univ. Press, Delhi, 1991.

——. "Tribal Identity and Class Differentiations: A Caste Study of the Chandhari Tribe", *Economic and Political Weekly,* Vol.14, No.7 & 8, Feb. 1979, Annual Number, pp. 459-64.

Shanin, Teodor (ed). *Peasants and Peasant Societies Selected Readings,* Penguin, Middlesex, England, 1971.

Singh, K. Suresh (ed). *The Tribal Situation in India,* Indian Institute of Advanced Studies, Shimla, Motilal Banarsidan, Delhi, 1992.

——. *Tribal Society in India An Anthropo-Historical Perspective,* Manohar, New Delhi, 1985.

——. *Economies of the Tribes and their Transformation.* Concept Pub., New Delhi, 1982.

Sinha, Surajit. "Tribal Solidarity Movements in India", *in ed.* B. Chaudhuri *Tribal Development, op. cit.*

-----. "Tribe-Caste and Peasant-Caste Continua in Central India", *Man in India,* 1965, Vol. 45., No.1, pp. 57-83.

Sirsalkar, P.R. "Primitive Tribes: Challenge for Development", *Tribal Research Bulletin,* Vol.7, No.2, March 1985, pp.7-8.

Srinivas, M.N. et al. eds., *The Fieldworker and the Field: Problems and Challenges in Sociological Investigation,* Oxford University Press, New Delhi, 1979.

Raigad Zilla Gazetteer, Maharastra Shasan, Bombay 1993 (Marathi).

Telageri, Srikant, G. *The Aryan Invasion Theory and Indian Nationalism,* Aditya Prakashan, New Delhi, 1993.

Tribhuwan, Peters. "Medico-Ethnobiology of the Katkaris and Thakkurs", *Tribal Research Bulletin,* Vol.14, No.1, March,

1992, pp. 20-4.

Vidyarthi, L.P. *Strategy for Tribal Development in India: Proceedings of the Seminar on Tribal Development,* Bhubaneshwar, 1975.

Vohra, Gautam. *Age at Marriage and Child Survival Measures among Katkari and Thakkar Adivasis,* Population Education Resource Centre, SNDT Univ, Bombay, Mimeograph, 1991.

Vyas N.N. "Kathodi- A Tribe in Transition", in N.N. Vyas and R.S. Mann eds., *Indian Tribes in Transition,* Rawat Pub. Jaipur-Delhi, 1982.

Walt, George. *A Dictionary of Economic Products of India,* Cosmo, Bombay, 1972.

Weling, A.N. *The Kathkaris: A Sociological Study of an Aboriginal Tribe of the Bombay Presidency,* Bombay Book Depot, Bombay, 1934.

Wilson, John. "Account of the Waralis and Katodis—two of The Forest-Tribes of northern Konkan", *Royal Asiatic Society of Great Britain and Ireland, Journal,* Vol. 7, Serial No. 13, 1843, pp.14-31.

Winick, Charles. *Dictionary of Anthropology,* Peter Owen, London, 1960.

Zimmermann R. *The Khandala Katkaris,* British India Press, Mazagaon, Bombay, 1921.

INDEX